Learning AngularJS

Ken Williamson

Beijing · Cambridge · Farnham · Köln · Sebastopol · Tokyo    **O'REILLY®**

Learning AngularJS

by Ken Williamson

Printed in the United States of America.

Published by O'Reilly Media, Inc., 1005 Gravenstein Highway North, Sebastopol, CA 95472.

O'Reilly books may be purchased for educational, business, or sales promotional use. Online editions are also available for most titles (*http://safaribooksonline.com*). For more information, contact our corporate/institutional sales department: 800-998-9938 or *corporate@oreilly.com*.

Editor: Meg Foley	**Indexer:** WordCo. Indexing Services
Production Editor: Nicole Shelby	**Interior Designer:** David Futato
Copyeditor: Rachel Head	**Cover Designer:** Ellie Volckhausen
Proofreader: Rachel Monaghan	**Illustrator:** Rebecca Demarest

March 2015:   First Edition

Revision History for the First Edition
2015-03-10:   First Release

See *http://oreilly.com/catalog/errata.csp?isbn=9781491916759* for release details.

978-1-491-91675-9

[LSI]

I would like to thank my son Chris for all his help and for being a sounding board. Thanks, Chris.

Table of Contents

Preface

The world of software development has changed drastically over the last few decades. Many software methodologies and concepts that were considered "cutting edge" 20 or so years ago are now common practice in the field of software development, and have been for years. One example is the World Wide Web and the use of web browsers to deliver software to users. In 1993, the concept of delivering software over the Internet that could then run in a web browser on any machine running on any operating system was considered bleeding edge. But as any computer user knows, that practice has been commonplace for years now.

When JavaScript client-side web application frameworks like AngularJS, Backbone.js, and Ember.js first appeared, they were considered too cutting edge for most serious software projects. As they matured, however, software architects and developers saw great potential in these frameworks. Applications built with JavaScript client-side frameworks exist and run entirely on the user's hardware, much like conventional thick-client applications. Applications written using these frameworks are much faster than conventional web applications and provide a much better user experience.

Over the last couple of years, JavaScript client-side frameworks have made great strides in functionality and reliability, and they are now heavily used to build mobile HTML5 applications. But mobile applications are only the starting point. These frameworks now have the potential to radically change the way we build modern web application software. Of all the JavaScript frameworks available, AngularJS, backed by Google, is the one that shines the brightest.

AngularJS has many advantages over other JavaScript client-side frameworks. AngularJS uses the MVC design pattern and embraces that pattern completely. The model, view, and controller are all clearly defined in AngularJS and serve to greatly simplify the development process. With AngularJS, developers can build applications that have a clear separation between their functional layers.

One of the greatest advantages of AngularJS over other JavaScript client-side frameworks is the unique way in which it lets developers interact with RESTful web services. AngularJS's `resource` object lets developers interact with REST services like standard objects. The complexity of REST services can be greatly simplified using this approach: with only a few lines of code, you can create an AngularJS service that interacts with multiple backend REST services. Those services can then be used throughout your application, reducing the total number of lines of code.

In fact, one of the biggest advantages of AngularJS over other client-side frameworks is its concept of services. AngularJS services help to greatly simplify an application by compartmentalizing client-side logic into single units of code. Those single units, called services, can then be used repeatedly throughout an application. AngularJS services prove especially powerful when you're building large enterprise applications with many lines of code and much complexity. Complex logic can be written only once inside an AngularJS service and then used wherever needed. That alone makes AngularJS the best choice for your next JavaScript project.

Thanks to this use of services and its all-inclusive design, AngularJS helps developers write less code, thereby greatly reducing application complexity. The simplicity of AngularJS makes it easy to learn and easy to use. Any time spent learning AngularJS is time well spent. Any time spent developing AngularJS applications is time spent turning a cutting-edge technology into a commonplace technology. In this book I strive to help you do both, encouraging design concepts and practices that will help you build better AngularJS applications.

Why I Wrote This Book

I constantly see development teams avoid using AngularJS because of its perceived steep learning curve. Those same teams often choose other JavaScript frameworks because they initially seem easier to learn. But AngularJS is not hard to learn at all. It is actually much easier to learn than other JavaScript frameworks, if the learning process is approached correctly. Like many others, I struggled to learn AngularJS in the beginning. This book was written to help developers avoid the early struggles associated with learning AngularJS and get started building AngularJS applications and websites very quickly.

What This Book Covers

This book covers everything you need to know to build fully functional AngularJS applications. The book starts off with the basics of AngularJS. You will learn about AngularJS components in early chapters. As chapters progress, you will get hands-on experience building working AngularJS projects.

Near the end of the book, you will write the AngularJS part of a working MEAN stack blog application and deploy the application to the cloud. MEAN stands for MongoDB, ExpressJS, AngularJS, and Node.js. Many industry experts believe the MEAN stack will be a dominant web development platform in coming years.

After reading this book, you will have the knowledge to start building high-quality AngularJS applications and websites. You will also gain a clear understanding of the design concepts associated with AngularJS applications, and of security as it relates to AngularJS applications.

Who Should Read This Book

This book is intended for anyone who has an interest in learning to develop AngularJS applications or websites quickly. It will also be helpful to anyone interested in learning how AngularJS is used in a MEAN stack application. The reader will gain not only a conceptual understanding of AngularJS, but hands-on experience as well. Anyone reading this book should have some knowledge of JavaScript, software design concepts, and software design patterns. A prior knowledge of web development will also be helpful.

The Chapters in This Book

This book starts off with the very basics of AngularJS and assumes the reader has no prior knowledge of the framework. The chapters are arranged as follows:

- *Chapter 1, Introduction to AngularJS*, starts off with a basic introduction to AngularJS. It helps the reader understand how AngularJS differs from other frameworks.
- *Chapter 2, The IDE and AngularJS Projects*, covers setting up a development environment and building AngularJS projects. It also covers how to set up a test environment for AngularJS.
- *Chapter 3, MVC and AngularJS*, compares AngularJS to traditional web MVC frameworks. It shows why AngularJS is a better framework for building modern web applications and websites.
- *Chapter 4, AngularJS Controllers*, is a discussion of AngularJS controllers. The reader will build part of a working application and implement controller testing near the end of the chapter.
- *Chapter 5, AngularJS Views and Bootstrap*, covers AngularJS views built with Twitter Bootstrap. The reader will continue working on a functional application and implement testing.
- *Chapter 6, AngularJS and REST Services*, covers AngularJS services as they relate to REST services. The reader will continue working on the application and connect it to public REST services written for this book.

- *Chapter 7, AngularJS Models*, covers AngularJS models and how they relate to controllers and views. The reader will continue working on the application started earlier.
- *Chapter 8, Services and Business Logic*, covers non-REST AngularJS services. In this chapter the reader will build part of the security layer used later in the book.
- *Chapter 9, AngularJS Directives*, covers the basics of building and testing AngularJS directives.
- *Chapter 10, AngularJS Security*, shows the reader how to use the security layer introduced in Chapter 8 to secure the AngularJS application started earlier.
- *Chapter 11, MEAN Cloud and Mobile*, shows the reader how to use the AngularJS application developed in previous chapters in a MEAN stack application and in a mobile application.
- *Chapter 12, AngularJS and SEO*, covers search engine optimization as it relates to AngularJS applications and websites.

Conventions Used in This Book

The following typographical conventions are used in this book:

Italic
> Indicates new terms, URLs, email addresses, filenames, and file extensions.

`Constant width`
> Used for program listings, as well as within paragraphs to refer to program elements such as variable or function names, databases, data types, environment variables, statements, and keywords.

`Constant width bold`
> Shows commands or other text that should be typed literally by the user.

`Constant width italic`
> Shows text that should be replaced with user-supplied values or by values determined by context.

 This element signifies a general note.

 This element signifies a warning or caution.

Using Code Examples

Supplemental material (code examples, exercises, etc.) is available for download at *https://github.com/KenWilliamson*.

This book is here to help you get your job done. In general, if example code is offered with this book, you may use it in your programs and documentation. You do not need to contact us for permission unless you're reproducing a significant portion of the code. For example, writing a program that uses several chunks of code from this book does not require permission. Selling or distributing a CD-ROM of examples from O'Reilly books does require permission. Answering a question by citing this book and quoting example code does not require permission. Incorporating a significant amount of example code from this book into your product's documentation does require permission.

We appreciate, but do not require, attribution. An attribution usually includes the title, author, publisher, and ISBN. For example: "*Learning AngularJS* by Ken Williamson (O'Reilly). Copyright 2015 Ken Williamson, 978-1-491-91675-9."

If you feel your use of code examples falls outside fair use or the permission given above, feel free to contact us at *permissions@oreilly.com*.

Safari® Books Online

 *Safari Books Online* is an on-demand digital library that delivers expert content in both book and video form from the world's leading authors in technology and business.

Technology professionals, software developers, web designers, and business and creative professionals use Safari Books Online as their primary resource for research, problem solving, learning, and certification training.

Safari Books Online offers a range of plans and pricing for enterprise, government, education, and individuals.

Members have access to thousands of books, training videos, and prepublication manuscripts in one fully searchable database from publishers like O'Reilly Media, Prentice Hall Professional, Addison-Wesley Professional, Microsoft Press, Sams, Que, Peachpit Press, Focal Press, Cisco Press, John Wiley & Sons, Syngress, Morgan Kaufmann, IBM Redbooks, Packt, Adobe Press, FT Press, Apress, Manning, New Riders, McGraw-Hill, Jones & Bartlett, Course Technology, and hundreds more. For more information about Safari Books Online, please visit us online.

How to Contact Us

Please address comments and questions concerning this book to the publisher:

O'Reilly Media, Inc.
1005 Gravenstein Highway North
Sebastopol, CA 95472
800-998-9938 (in the United States or Canada)
707-829-0515 (international or local)
707-829-0104 (fax)

We have a web page for this book, where we list errata, examples, and any additional information. You can access this page at *http://bit.ly/learning-angularjs*.

To comment or ask technical questions about this book, send email to *bookquestions@oreilly.com*.

For more information about our books, courses, conferences, and news, see our website at *http://www.oreilly.com*.

Find us on Facebook: *http://facebook.com/oreilly*

Follow us on Twitter: *http://twitter.com/oreillymedia*

Watch us on YouTube: *http://www.youtube.com/oreillymedia*

Introduction to AngularJS

Google's AngularJS is an all-inclusive JavaScript model-view-controller (MVC) framework that makes it very easy to quickly build applications that run well on any desktop or mobile platform. In a very short period of time, AngularJS has moved from being an unknown open source offering to one of the best known and most widely used JavaScript client-side frameworks offered. AngularJS 1.3 and greater combined with jQuery and Twitter Bootstrap give you everything you need to rapidly build HTML5 JavaScript application frontends that use REST web services for the backend processes. This book will show you how to use all three frontend components to harness the power of REST services on the backend and quickly build powerful mobile and desktop applications.

JavaScript Client-Side Frameworks

JavaScript client-side applications run on the user's device or PC, and therefore shift the workload to the user's hardware and away from the server. Until fairly recently, server-side web MVC frameworks like Struts, Spring MVC, and ASP.NET were the frameworks of choice for most web-based software development projects. JavaScript client-side frameworks, however, are sustainable models that offer many advantages over conventional web frameworks, such as simplicity, rapid development, speed of operation, testability, and the ability to package the entire application and deploy it to all mobile devices and the Web with relative ease. You can build your application one time and deploy and run it anywhere, on any platform, with no modifications. That's powerful.

AngularJS makes that process even faster and easier. It helps you build frontend applications in days rather than months and has complete support for unit testing to help reduce quality assurance (QA) time. AngularJS has a rich set of user documentation and great community support to help answer questions during your development process. Models and views in AngularJS are much simpler than what you find in most JavaScript client-side frameworks. Controllers, often missing in other Java-Script client-side frameworks, are key functional components in AngularJS.

Figure 1-1 shows a diagram of an AngularJS application and all related MVC components. Once the AngularJS application is launched, the model, view, controller, and all HTML documents are loaded on the user's mobile or desktop device and run entirely on the user's hardware. As you can see, calls are made to the backend REST services, where all business logic and business processes are located. The backend REST services can be located on a private web server or in the cloud (which is most often the case). Cloud REST services can scale from a handful of users to millions of users with relative ease.

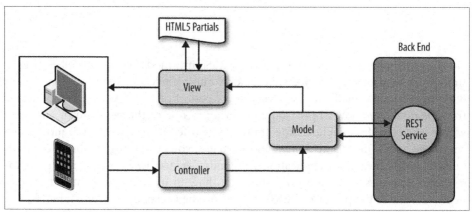

Figure 1-1. Diagram of an AngularJS MVC application

Single-Page Applications

AngularJS is most often used to build applications that conform to the single-page application (SPA) concept. SPAs are applications that have one entry point HTML page; all the application content is dynamically added to and removed from that one page. You can see the entry point of our SPA in the *index.html* code that follows. The tag `<div ng-view></div>` is where all dynamic content is inserted into *index.html*:

```
<!-- chapter1/index.html -->
<!DOCTYPE html>

<html lang="en" ng-app="helloWorldApp">

<head>

<title>AngularJS Hello World</title>

<meta name="viewport" content="width=device-width, initial-scale=1.0">
<meta http-equiv="Content-Type" content="text/html; charset=UTF-8">
```

```
<script src="js/libs/angular.min.js"></script>
<script src="js/libs/angular-route.min.js"></script>
<script src="js/libs/angular-resource.min.js"></script>
<script src="js/libs/angular-cookies.min.js"></script>


<script src="js/app.js"></script>
<script src="js/controllers.js"></script>
<script src="js/services.js"></script>


</head>

<body>
<div ng-view></div>
</body>

</html>
```

As the user clicks on links in the application, existing content attached to the tag is removed and new dynamic content is then attached to the same tag. Rather than the user waiting for a new page to load, new content is dynamically displayed in a fraction of the time that it would take to load a new HTML web page.

You can download the source for the Chapter 1 "Hello, World" application from GitHub (*http://bit.ly/lajs-github*).

Bootstrapping the Application

Bootstrapping AngularJS is the process of loading AngularJS when an application first starts. Loading the AngularJS libraries in a page will start the bootstrap process. The *index.html* file is analyzed, and the parser looks for the ng-app tag. The line <html lang="en" ng-app="helloWorldApp"></html> shows how ng-app is defined. The following code shows the JavaScript that is fired by that line in the *index.html* file. As you can see, *app.js* is where the AngularJS application *helloWorldApp* is defined as an AngularJS module, and this is the entry point into the application. The variable hello WorldApp in this file could be named anything. I will, however, call it helloWorldApp for the sake of uniformity:

```
/* chapter1/app.js excerpt */
'use strict';
/* App Module */

var helloWorldApp = angular.module('helloWorldApp', [
```

```
    'ngRoute',
    'helloWorldControllers'
]);
```

Dependency Injection

Dependency injection (DI) is a design pattern where dependencies are defined in an application as part of the configuration. Dependency injection helps you avoid having to manually create application dependencies. AngularJS uses dependency injection to load module dependencies when an application first starts. The *app.js* code in the previous section shows how AngularJS dependencies are defined.

As you can see, two dependencies are defined as needed by the *helloWorldApp* application at startup. The dependencies are defined in an array in the module definition. The first dependency is the AngularJS ngRoute module, which provides routing to the application. The second dependency is our controller module, helloWorldCon trollers. We will cover controllers in depth later, but for now just understand that controllers are needed by our applications at startup time.

Dependency injection is not a new concept. It was introduced over 10 years ago and has been used consistently in various application frameworks; DI was at the core of the popular Spring framework written in Java. One of its main advantages is that it reduces the need for boilerplate code, writing of which would normally be a time-consuming process for a development team.

Dependency injection also helps to make an application more testable. That is one of the main advantages of using AngularJS to build JavaScript applications. AngularJS applications are much easier to test than applications written with most JavaScript frameworks. In fact, there is a test framework that has been specifically written to make testing AngularJS applications easy. We will talk more about testing at the end of this chapter.

AngularJS Routes

AngularJS routes are defined through the $routeProvider API. Routes are dependent on the ngRoute module, and that's why it is a requirement when the application starts. The following code from *app.js* shows how we define routes in an AngularJS application. Two routes are defined—the first is / and the second is */show*:

```
/* chapter1/app.js excerpt */
helloWorldApp.config(['$routeProvider', '$locationProvider',
function($routeProvider, $locationProvider){
  $routeProvider.
    when('/', {
      templateUrl: 'partials/main.html',
      controller: 'MainCtrl' }).
```

```
    when('/show', {
        templateUrl: 'partials/show.html',
        controller: 'ShowCtrl'
});
```

The two defined routes map directly to URLs defined in the application. If a user clicks on a link in the application specified as *www.someDomainName/show*, the */show* route will be followed and the content associated with that URL will be displayed. If the user clicks on a link specified as *www.someDomainName/*, the / route will be followed and that content will be displayed.

HTML5 Mode

The complete *app.js* file is shown next. The last line in *app.js* ($locationPro vider.html5Mode(false).hashPrefix('!');) uses the locationProvider service. This line of code turns off the HTML5 mode and turns on the hashbang mode of AngularJS. If you were to turn on HTML5 mode instead by passing true, the application would use the HTML5 History API. HTML5 mode also gives the application pretty URLs like */someAppName/blogPost/5* instead of the standard AngularJS URLs like */someAppName/#!/blogPost/5* that use the #!, known as the hashbang.

```
/* chapter1/app.js complete file */

'use strict';
/* App Module */

var helloWorldApp = angular.module('helloWorldApp', [
  'ngRoute',
  'helloWorldControllers'
]);

helloWorldApp.config(['$routeProvider', '$locationProvider',
  function($routeProvider, $locationProvider) {
    $routeProvider.
      when('/', {
        templateUrl: 'partials/main.html',
        controller: 'MainCtrl'
      }).when('/show', {
        templateUrl: 'partials/show.html',
        controller: 'ShowCtrl'
});
    $locationProvider.html5Mode(false).hashPrefix('!');
}]);
```

HTML5 mode can provide pretty URLs, but it does require configuration changes on the web server in most cases. The changes are different for each individual web server, and can differ for different server installations as well. HTML5 mode also handles URL changes in a different way, by using the HTML History API for navigation.

Using HTML5 mode is just a configuration change in AngularJS, and we won't cover the needed server changes in this book as our focus is on AngularJS. The AngularJS site has documentation on the changes needed for all modern web servers when HTML5 mode is enabled. Using this mode has some benefits, but we will stick with hashbang mode in our chapter exercises.

Hashbang mode is used to support conventional search engines that don't have the ability to execute JavaScript on Ajax sites like those built with AngularJS. When a conventional search engine searches a site built with AngularJS that uses hashbangs, the search engine replaces the *#!* with *?_escaped_fragment_=*. Conventional search engines expect the server to have HTML snapshots at the location where *_escaped_fragment_=* is configured to point. HTML snapshots are merely copies of the HTML rendered version of the website or application.

Modern Search Engines

Fortunately, modern search engines have the ability to execute JavaScript, as announced by Google in a news release on May 23, 2014 (*http://bit.ly/1EWcX3P*). Hashbang mode also allows AngularJS applications to store Ajax requested pages in the browser's history. That process often simplifies browser bookmarks.

AngularJS Templates

AngularJS partials, also called *templates*, are code sections that contain HTML code that are bound to the <div ng-view></div></div> tag shown in the *index.html* file earlier in this chapter. If you look back at the complete *app.js* file, you can see that different templateUrl values are defined for each route.

The *main.html* and *show.html* files listed next show the two defined partials (templates). The templates contain just HTML code, with nothing special at this time. Later, we will use AngularJS's built-in template language to display dynamic data in our templates:

```
<!-- chapter1/main.html -->

<div>Hello World</div>

<!-- chapter1/show.html -->

<div>Show The World</div>
```

As the user clicks on the different links, the value assigned to <div ng-view> is replaced with the content of the associated template files. The value of *controller* defined for each route references the controller component (of the MVC pattern) that is defined for each particular route.

The next sections provide a brief overview of each AngularJS MVC component and how it is used, to give you a better understanding of how AngularJS works. Unlike most JavaScript client-side frameworks, AngularJS provides the model, view, and controller components for use in all applications. That often helps developers familiar with design patterns to quickly grasp AngularJS concepts.

AngularJS Views (MVC)

Many JavaScript client-side frameworks require you to actually define the view classes in JavaScript, and they can contain anywhere from a few to hundreds of lines of code. Such is not the case with AngularJS. AngularJS pulls in all the templates defined for an application and builds the views in the document object model (DOM) for you. Therefore, the only work you need to do to build the views is to create the templates.

Building views in AngularJS is a simple process that uses mostly HTML and CSS. The simplicity of AngularJS views is a huge time-saver when you're building AngularJS applications. We will cover creating templates in more detail in Chapter 5.

AngularJS Models (MVC)

Many JavaScript client-side frameworks also require you to create JavaScript model classes. That is also not the case with AngularJS. AngularJS has a $scope object that is used to store the application model. Scopes are attached to the DOM. The way to access the model is by using data properties assigned to the $scope object.

The AngularJS $scope helps to simplify JavaScript applications considerably. Other JavaScript frameworks often encourage placing large amounts of business logic inside the model classes for the particular framework. Unfortunately, that practice often leads to duplicated business logic. In a large project, that can lead to thousands of lines of useless code. We will talk more about models in Chapter 7.

AngularJS Controllers (MVC)

AngularJS controllers are the tape that holds the models and views together. The controller is where you should place all business logic specific to a particular view when it's not possible to place the logic inside a REST service. Business logic should almost always be placed in backend REST services whenever possible; this helps to simplify AngularJS applications.

When business logic placed inside an application is used by multiple controllers, it should be placed in AngularJS non-REST services instead. Those services can then be injected into any controller that needs access to the logic. We will cover non-REST services in Chapter 8 in great detail.

Controller Business Logic

The following code shows the contents of the *controllers.js* file. At the start of the file we define the `helloWorldController` module. We then define two new controllers, `MainCtrl` and `ShowCtrl`, and attach them to the `helloWorldController` module. Business logic specific to the `MainCtrl` controller is defined inside that controller. Likewise, business logic specific to the `ShowCtrl` controller is defined inside the `ShowCtrl` controller. Notice that `$scope` is injected into both controllers. The `$scope` that is injected into each controller is specific to that controller and not visible to other controllers:

```
/* chapter1/controllers.js */

'use strict';
/* Controllers */

var helloWorldControllers =
angular.module('helloWorldControllers', []);

helloWorldControllers.controller('MainCtrl', ['$scope',
function MainCtrl($scope) {
  $scope.message = "Hello World";
}]);

helloWorldControllers.controller('ShowCtrl', ['$scope',
function ShowCtrl($scope) {
  $scope.message = "Show The World";
}]);
```

As you can see, we are now using the model to populate the messages that get displayed in the templates. The following code shows the modified templates that use the newly created model values. The line `$scope.message = "Hello World"` in the `MainCtrl` controller is used to create a property named `message` that is added to the scope (which holds the model attributes). We then use the double curly braces markup (`{{}}`) inside the *main.html* template to gain access to and display the value assigned to `$scope.message`:

```
<!-- chapter1/main.html -->

<div>{{message}}</div>
```

Using double curly braces is AngularJS's way of displaying scope properties in the view. The double curly braces syntax is actually part of the built-in AngularJS template language.

Likewise, we use the value assigned to the `message` property with the line `$scope.mes sage = "Show The World"` in the `ShowCtrl` controller to populate the message displayed in the *show.html* template. We use the double curly braces markup inside the *show.html* template as before to gain access to and display the model property:

```
<!-- chapter1/show.html -->

<div>{{message}}</div>
```

Integrating AngularJS with Other Frameworks

AngularJS can be integrated into existing applications that use other frameworks. Those may be other JavaScript client-side frameworks, or web frameworks like Spring MVC or CakePHP. You could take an application written in Java and add some new client-side functionality very easily using AngularJS, cutting development time considerably.

Adding a new AngularJS shopping cart to an existing Java application would be a good example to consider. The existing Java application could be written with the Spring framework and use Spring MVC as the web framework. Adding a shopping cart built with Java using Spring MVC could be a time-consuming process. That, however, would not be the case with AngularJS.

You could quickly build a shopping cart with AngularJS and be up and running in a few hours, easily integrating the cart into the existing Java application. Not only would you be able to build the cart faster, but you could quickly add unit testing to increase coverage and reduce the application's defects. AngularJS was designed to be testable from the very beginning; that is one of the key features of AngularJS and a major reason for selecting it over other JavaScript client-side frameworks. We will talk about testing AngularJS applications in the next section.

Testing AngularJS Applications

In recent years continuous integration (CI) build tools such as Travis CI, Jenkins, and others have risen in popularity and usage. CI tools have the ability to run test scripts during a build process and give immediate feedback by way of test results. CI tools help to automate the process of testing software and can often alert developers of software defects as soon as they occur.

There are two types of AngularJS tests that integrate well with CI tools. The first type of testing is unit testing. Most developers are familiar with unit testing; they can often identify software defects early in the development process by testing small units of code. The second type of testing is end-to-end (E2E) testing. E2E testing helps to identify software defects by testing how software components connect and interact.

There are many testing tools used for unit testing AngularJS applications. Two of the most popular are Karma and JS Test Driver. Karma, however, is quickly becoming the top choice for AngularJS development teams. The most popular E2E test tool for end-to-end testing of AngularJS applications is a new tool called Protractor. Both tools integrate well with CI build tools.

Large AngularJS development teams will find testing AngularJS applications with continuous integration tools to be a huge time-saver. Often a failed CI test is the first indication of a defect for large teams. Small teams will also see many advantages to CI-based testing. AngularJS developers should always develop both unit tests and end-to-end tests whenever possible.

Throughout this book, we will cover both unit testing and end-to-end testing. We will use both Karma and JsTestDrive for unit testing, and we will use Protractor for E2E testing.

Conclusion

We will cover models, views, and controllers in great detail in later chapters, using those components to build working applications that show the power of AngularJS. We will show how all three components work together to simplify the job of building JavaScript client-side applications. We will also cover building both unit tests and end-to-end tests for AngularJS applications.

Chapter 2 will focus on helping you set up a development environment for HTML5. We will also download the latest versions of AngularJS, jQuery, and Twitter Bootstrap and add those to our sample project.

The IDE and AngularJS Projects

Many JavaScript editors are used by AngularJS developers. Using an integrated development environment (IDE) with a good JavaScript editor is a huge time-saver and speeds up the development process considerably. IDEs with good JavaScript tools usually have good HTML5 and CSS3 tools as well, which helps to increase a developer's productivity substantially. We will harness the power of an IDE in this book.

The IDE

We will be using NetBeans as our integrated development environment. You can, however, use any IDE or editor that you prefer. Most of this chapter will be generic and will work fine with any modern IDE. To get started, do the following:

1. Download and install the latest version of NetBeans from the NetBeans website (*https://netbeans.org/downloads*) (or download another IDE of your choice).

2. Download (*https://angularjs.org*) the latest versions of the following AngularJS files:

    a. *angular.min.js* (main libs)

    b. *angular-route.min.js* (routing libs)

    c. *angular-cookies.min.js* (cookie libs)

    d. *angular-resource.min.js* (REST service libs)

3. Download (*http://jquery.com/download*) the latest version of jQuery.

4. Download (*http://getbootstrap.com/getting-started/#download*) the latest version of Twitter Bootstrap.

Start NetBeans and create a new HTML5 project, as shown in Figure 2-1. Name the project *AngularJsHelloWorld_chapter2*.

Figure 2-1. Creating your new HTML5 project

Now do the following:

1. Create the directory structure shown in Figure 2-2 under *Site Root*.

2. Copy the AngularJS, jQuery, and Bootstrap files into the *libs* folder.

3. Right-click the *js* folder and create the following *.js* files:
   a. *app.js* (where the application is defined)
   b. *controllers.js* (where controllers are defined)
   c. *services.js* (where services are defined)
   d. *main.html* under the *partials* folder
   e. *show.html* under the *partials* folder
   f. *index.html* under the *Site Root* folder

Figure 2-2. Creating the directory structure

Editing the HTML Code

Now we must edit the *index.html* file to create bootstrapping for the application and to use the libraries and *.js* files just added. Edit your newly created *index.html* file to match the code that follows. These are all the changes that we need to make to this file for now. Next, we will edit the *app.js* and *controllers.js* files:

```
<!-- chapter2/index.html -->

<!DOCTYPE html>

<html lang="en" ng-app="helloWorldApp">

<head>

<title>AngularJS Hello World</title>
<meta name="viewport" content="width=device-width,
    initial-scale=1.0">
<meta http-equiv="Content-Type" content="text/html; charset=UTF-8">
<script src="js/libs/jquery-1.10.2.min.js"></script>
<script src="js/libs/angular.min.js"></script>
<script src="js/libs/angular-route.min.js"></script>
<script src="js/libs/angular-resource.min.js"></script>
<script src="js/libs/angular-cookies.min.js"></script>
<script src="js/app.js"></script>
<script src="js/controllers.js"></script>
<script src="js/services.js"></script>

</head>

<body>
<div ng-view></div>
</body>

</html>
```

Editing the JavaScript Code

Update your newly created *app.js* file with the code shown here. As you can see, it is the same code we covered in Chapter 1:

```
/* chapter2/app.js */

'use strict';
/* App Module */

var helloWorldApp = angular.module('helloWorldApp', [
  'ngRoute',
  'helloWorldControllers'
]);
```

```
helloWorldApp.config(['$routeProvider', '$locationProvider',
function($routeProvider, $locationProvider) {
  $routeProvider.
    when('/', {
    templateUrl: 'partials/main.html',
    controller: 'MainCtrl'
  }).when('/show', {
    templateUrl: 'partials/show.html',
    controller: 'ShowCtrl'
});


$locationProvider.html5Mode(false).hashPrefix('!');
}]);
```

Likewise, update your newly created *controllers.js* file with the code shown next. This is also the same code covered in Chapter 1 for the controller:

```
/* chapter2/controllers.js */

'use strict';
/* Controllers */

var helloWorldControllers =
  angular.module('helloWorldControllers', []);
helloWorldControllers.controller('MainCtrl',
  ['$scope', '$location', '$http',
function MainCtrl($scope, $location, $http) {
  $scope.message = "Hello World";
}]);

helloWorldControllers.controller('ShowCtrl',
  ['$scope', '$location', '$http',
function ShowCtrl($scope, $location, $http) {
  $scope.message = "Show The World";
}]);
```

Creating the Templates

Now all that is left is to create the templates (partials). Do the following:

```
<!-- chapter2/main.html -->

<div>{{message}}</div>
```

1. Edit the new *main.html* and add the code shown here:

2. Edit *show.html* and add the code shown here:

```
<!-- chapter2/show.html -->

<div>{{message}}</div>
```

Running the Applications

That concludes the code changes needed in the Chapter 2 project for now. Right-click on the new HTML5 project and select "Run." At the URL *http://localhost:8383/AngularJsHelloWorld_chapter2/index.html#!/*, you should see the words "Hello World" in the top-left corner of the browser.

Now change the URL to *http://localhost:8383/AngularJsHelloWorld_chapter2/index.html#!/show*, and you should see the words "Show The World" in the top-left corner of the browser. If you get the correct results, your project is configured correctly. If you get a different result, go back through this chapter and verify that you completed all the steps.

If you continue to have problems, download the Chapter 2 source from GitHub (*http://bit.ly/lajs-github*) and try to run that code.

Testing AngularJS Applications in the IDE

As I mentioned in the previous chapter, there are two types of tests that are used for testing AngularJS applications. The first type of test is the unit test. Unit testing is usually the first place where issues with the code are found, through testing small units of code. The second type of test is end-to-end (E2E) testing. E2E testing helps to identify software defects by testing how components connect and interact together as a whole.

NetBeans can easily work with both JsTestDriver and Karma for unit testing AngularJS applications. Karma is quickly becoming the most popular choice for AngularJS development teams, so we will focus more on Karma in later chapters. Protractor is the most popular test framework for E2E testing of AngularJS applications. Currently, most development environments don't have built-in support for Protractor. Protractor is a new testing framework, and it may take a while before most IDEs and editors support it. NetBeans currently has no support for Protractor.

Both Karma and Protractor run on Node.js. Node.js is an open source cross-platform framework built on the Google V8 JavaScript engine. We will use Node.js later in this book, when we focus on building MEAN stack applications. Installing Karma and Protractor is a relatively easy process that uses the Node.js package manager (npm) for the installation process.

Node.js-based projects use a JSON file named *package.json* as the project configuration file. The following is a standard *package.json* file used in a NetBeans project. If you look at the dependencies section of the file, you will see that we actually define Karma as a dependency of the application. That is because Karma is usually installed locally at the project level for each individual project:

```
{"chapter": 2, "name": "package.json"},

{
  "name" : "UlboraCmsMean",
  "version" : "2.0.0",
  "description" : "UlboraCms",
  "keywords" : [ "Ulbora CMS", "Node.js", "Ken",
    "Williamson", "micbutton.com" ],
  "author" : {
    "name" : "Ken Williamson",
    "email" : "sales@drivensolutions.com",
    "url" : "http://www.drivensolutions.com/"
  },

  "homepage" : "http://www.ulboracms.org",
  "repository" : {
    "type" : "git",
    "url" : "https://github.com/Ulbora/ulboracms"
  },

  "engines" : {
    "node" : ">= 0.6.0",
    "npm" : ">= 1.0.0"
  },

  "dependencies" : {
    "express" : "~3.4.4",
    "mongoose" : "*",
    "atob": "*",
    "btoa": "*",
    "node-rest-client": "*",
    "consolidate": "*",
    "ejs": "*",
    "handlebars": "*",
    "nodemailer": "*",
    "karma": "*"
  },

  "bundleDependencies" : [ ],
  "private" : true,
  "main" : "./server.js",
  "bugs" : {
    "url" : "null"
  }
}
```

A file similar to this one will be used later in the book when we build the MEAN stack blog application. NetBeans, using a Node.js plugin, can generate the *package.json* file for you. The generated file will need to be modified to include the specifics of your particular project.

You can also use `npm init` to generate the *package.json* file. After typing `npm init` at the command prompt, you will be presented with a few questions. Your responses will then be used to create a default *package.json* file.

JsTestRunner

NetBeans has built-in support for JsTestRunner. The JsTestRunner configuration file can be generated and requires few changes to get unit testing running on your local environment.

Unlike Karma, JsTestRunner is not based on Node.js. The following is a standard JsTestRunner configuration file created by NetBeans for an AngularJS project. Notice in the first line that the test server URL and port are specified:

```
/* chapter2/jsTestDriver.conf */

server: http://localhost:42442
load:
  - test/lib/jasmine/jasmine.js
  - test/lib/jasmine-jstd-adapter/JasmineAdapter.js

  - public_html/js/libs/angular.min.js
  - public_html/js/libs/angular-mocks.js
  - public_html/js/libs/angular-cookies.min.js
  - public_html/js/libs/angular-resource.min.js
  - public_html/js/libs/angular-route.min.js
  - public_html/js/*.js

  - test/unit/*.js

exclude:
```

The locations of the test library files are specified under `load`. We also specify the locations of each unit test script that should be run by JsTestDriver. Test filenames usually end with "Spec." The following code shows a test specification file used to test AngularJS controllers. We will cover test specification in later chapters, when we run our first unit tests:

```
/* chapter2/controllerSpec.js */

/* Jasmine specs for controllers go here */
describe('Hello World', function() {

  beforeEach(module('helloWorldApp'));

  describe('MainCtrl', function(){
    var scope, ctrl;
```

```
beforeEach(inject(function($rootScope, $controller) {


  scope = $rootScope.$new();
  ctrl = $controller('MainCtrl', {$scope: scope});
})));

  it('should create initialed message', function() {
    expect(scope.message).toEqual("Hello World");
  });
});

describe('ShowCtrl', function(){
  var scope, ctrl;

  beforeEach(inject(function($rootScope, $controller) {
   scope = $rootScope.$new();
   ctrl = $controller('ShowCtrl', {$scope: scope});
  })));

  it('should create initialed message', function() {
    expect(scope.message).toEqual("Show The World");
  });

});

describe('CustomerCtrl', function(){
  var scope, ctrl;

  beforeEach(inject(function($rootScope, $controller) {
   scope = $rootScope.$new();
   ctrl = $controller('CustomerCtrl', {$scope: scope});
  })));

  it('should create initialed message', function() {
    expect(scope.customerName).toEqual("Bob's Burgers");
  });

});
});
```

Currently one of the big disadvantages of testing JavaScript applications is the lack of tools that generate test scripts based on the actual source files that need to be tested. Those tools have existed in the Java world for years, but they are still relatively non-existent in the realm of JavaScript. So, a file like this one needs to be created by hand to unit test each AngularJS controller.

Karma Test Runner

As I mentioned earlier, Karma is a test runner based on Node.js. The Karma team recommends installing Karma locally at the project level. So, we will add Karma in the *package.json* file of each of our projects, then use the following command to pull down and install Karma on a per-project basis:

```
npm install
```

When you run this command, npm reads the *package.json* file and installs the packages defined in the dependencies section of the file. After you run the command, Karma will be located under the *node_modules* folder within your project folder. Any other Node.js dependencies defined in the *package.json* file will also be located under the *node_modules* folder.

Karma requires a configuration file named *karma.conf.js* that specifies how it should run unit tests. You can use NetBeans to generate the *karma.conf.js* file. The following code shows a Karma configuration file generated by NetBeans. You can see there are sections of the file to specify the locations of library files, test scripts, and browser plugins:

```
/* chapter2/karma.conf.js  */

/*
 * To change this license header, choose License Headers in
 * Project Properties.
 * To change this template file, choose Tools -> Templates
 * and open the template in the editor.
 */

module.exports = function (config) {
    config.set({
        basePath: '../',
        files: [
        ],
        exclude: [
        ],
        autoWatch: true,
        frameworks: [
        ],
        browsers: [
        ],
        plugins: [
        ]
    });
};
```

We will cover Karma in more detail when we run our first unit test using Karma, in Chapter 4.

Protractor

Most development environments do not yet have built-in support for Protractor. Protractor is a Node.js-based framework, just like Karma. The installation process is much like the process for Karma. Protractor is built on top of WebDriverJS. The Protractor team recommends installing Protractor globally on your system.

To install Protractor on your development machine, issue the following command. Notice the -g flag in the command line—that tells npm to install Protractor globally for all projects and applications to use:

```
npm install -g protractor
```

Since Protractor is built on WebDriverJS, we must also configure WebDriverJS for our test environment. Run this command to update WebDriverJS with all the latest binaries:

```
webdriver-manager update
```

Once that command executes successfully, run the following command to start the Selenium Server that WebDriverJS uses to run Protractor test scripts:

```
webdriver-manager start
```

Protractor needs a configuration file that tells it how to run test scripts. Here are the contents of the *conf.js* file used to configure Protractor:

```
/* chapter2/conf.js Protractor configuration file */

exports.config = {
  seleniumAddress: 'http://localhost:4444/wd/hub',
  specs: ['blog-spec.js']
};
```

Once Protractor is installed and configured on your system, all that is left is to create the test scripts (test specifications) and run the scripts. Here's a sample script for a Protractor test:

```
/* chapter2/blog-spec.js */

describe('MEAN Blog', function() {

it('test the MEAN Blog', function() {

  browser.get('http://localhost:8080');

  element(by.model('blogList')).
    sendKeys('this is a blog post');

  element(by.css('[value="add"]')).click();

  var blogList = element.all(by.repeater('blog in blogs'));
```

```
expect(blogList.count()).toEqual(3);

expect(blogList.get(2).getText()).
  toEqual('this is a blog post');

  });
});
```

To run Protractor, issue the following command. Once you run the command, the browser window should open and display the test results:

```
protractor conf.js
```

Both Karma and Protractor can be integrated with continuous integration (CI) build systems like Travis CI and Jenkins, as I mentioned in Chapter 1. Many open source projects and enterprise development teams are moving toward CI build systems. Building Karma and Protractor testing into your AngularJS project is a vital part of the software development process. Time spent writing test scripts will ultimately be worth the effort in the long run.

We will cover both Karma and Protractor testing in great detail in later chapters. At that time we will install and configure both Karma and Protractor. Since both run on Node.js, you will also need to install that and the Node.js package manager (npm) on your system to power the test platforms.

Conclusion

In this chapter, we covered how to set up a development environment for AngularJS and built and ran a project with AngularJS. We also covered how to install a test environment with both JsTestDriver and Karma for unit testing our AngularJS projects. Finally, we looked at how to install and configure Protractor for doing end-to-end testing of AngularJS projects. With the knowledge gained from this chapter, we are ready to start working with more complex projects.

We are now ready to move on to Chapter 3, where we will cover MVC as it applies to AngularJS in more detail.

MVC and AngularJS

AngularJS presents a new and powerful way to develop web applications and websites—it has the power and functionality of conventional web frameworks, but with many advantages. AngularJS provides a way to build web apps and sites without the overhead normally associated with web frameworks.

Conventional web frameworks often tolerate server-side page scripting using PHP, Active Server Pages (ASP), and Java Server Pages (JSP). While server-side page scripting works sufficiently well on the server side, it does pose many maintenance issues for developers. But that is not the biggest issue with conventional web frameworks. Conventional web frameworks tend to run slower and be sluggish on mobile devices. And mobile users have a much lower tolerance for system delays and slow page loads than desktop users.

We must compare conventional web frameworks to AngularJS to understand the advantages that AngularJS presents. The next section will give you a clear understanding of the advantages of AngularJS over frameworks that you may have used in the past. With that understanding, we will be set to start building more maintainable applications in a better way.

The Old Way

Web MVC frameworks such as Apache Struts, Spring MVC, and the Zend Framework dominated the web development framework space for more than 15 years. Those same frameworks still dominate the space even today. There are some cases where web frameworks do present a better application design than more modern client-side frameworks, but those cases have diminished considerably over the last couple of years.

Web MVC frameworks reside entirely on the server. All functions such as database access, business logic, display logic, and UI activities happen on the server, using server memory and resources. Web MVC frameworks often use various page scripting techniques such as ASP, JSP, and PHP to control presentation logic, and in some cases business logic is also placed inside the pages.

Figure 3-1 shows a diagram of a conventional web MVC framework. From the diagram, you can see that the application or website runs on the backend server, and only the web browser runs on the user's hardware. Although the design in Figure 3-1 is old technology, it is still in heavy use today.

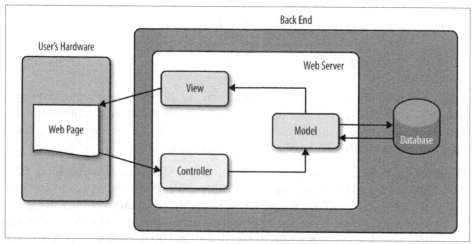

Figure 3-1. Conventional web MVC framework

Web applications and sites built with Ruby on Rails, the Zend Framework, Spring MVC, CakePHP, and other web frameworks are based on this design. Although the design works well in many situations, it does have several flaws.

One such design flaw is related to mobile applications and mobile websites. While web pages associated with web frameworks can be designed with HTML5 and CSS3 and be made responsive and look good on mobile devices, the application or website is dependent on the web server to make the different pages available to the mobile device. In addition, the web pages must run in the mobile device's web browser.

The application or site developer has very little control over the mobile device's web browser. A user must find the site or application and enter its URL into the browser's address bar in order to view the web page or to run the application. Mobile users, however, often find that process too time-consuming.

While mobile sites and applications distributed as web-based designs have the advantage of saving development hours and money, they do pose a problem in many situations. Often, mobile developers need to build custom device applications and have those applications distributed via the various online stores. Not only does a custom application offer a higher level of customer service, but it also serves as a marketing tool. As the number of mobile devices in use increases, the demand for custom mobile applications will also increase.

Consider, for example, a doctor's office that needs to allow patients to make appointments from their mobile devices. Such an application would need to be fast and have almost no delay when patients are navigating from page to page. The application would also need to look good on any device. A user with a small smartphone should have the same user experience as a user with a 10-inch tablet.

An application developer or architect attempting a mobile design based on the system design shown in Figure 3-1 really only has two choices to consider.

Choice One

The first option is to build a custom mobile application as a "wrapper" around the conventional site shown in Figure 3-1. Figure 3-2 shows an Android application designed as a wrapper application. As you can see, the Android application consists solely of an Android WebView component that is configured to point to the web application URL.

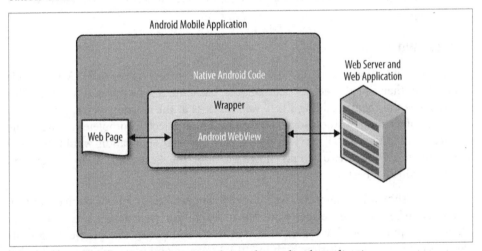

Figure 3-2. An Android wrapper around a traditional web application

The WebView component serves as a browser control inside the Android application. The developer can custom-configure the WebView component for the needs of the particular mobile application. All application operations still, however, run on the backend server (the web server), and the speed and responsiveness of the Android application are still highly dependent on that server and the quality of the user's Internet connection.

The following code shows a segment of an Android main `Activity`. A new Android `WebView` object is first instantiated. JavaScript is then enabled for the new instance. Finally, the URL of the website is loaded into the new instance with the `loadUrl` method:

```
/* chapter3 excerpt from an Android WebView shown loading a
 conventional website */

WebView webview = new WebView(this);

webview.getSettings().setJavaScriptEnabled(true);

final Activity activity = this;

webview.setWebViewClient(new WebViewClient() {

webview.loadUrl("http://www.google.com");
```

The `WebView` instance shown here is just a control for the device's internal web browser. The Android device's browser is completely dependent on the website for functionality. If the website that is linked to goes down or the network connection is lost, the user's browser will hang and completely stop working. That functionality is very frustrating for mobile device users. It is, however, a common configuration for mobile applications.

Choice Two

The second option would require the developer to write a native or HTML5 mobile application that called web services on the backend for business functions. This approach would require adding REST web services to the existing web application to make use of existing business logic. Option two is, in effect, a complete rewrite of the application. Adding REST services to the existing web application would not be a trivial matter. Option two would, however, offer the best application design and would provide the best user experience.

The design shown in Figure 3-1 isn't directly transferable to mobile devices. Fifteen years ago, when mobile devices were not in heavy use, that design was a common choice for application developers and architects, and posed few problems. Mobile device sales reached an all-time high in 2014, however, and most analysts predict that trend will only increase in the coming years.

Mobile is the future of everything. As wireless systems improve and evolve, mobile devices will evolve too and play a major role in all our daily activities. A mobile device will alert you when your table is ready at your favorite restaurant. That same device will replace your debit card or credit card when it's time to pay the bill and tip the server.

So, developers must plan for the future now. It's time to stop building software based on an old and outdated technology. That's where JavaScript client-side frameworks come into play, and that's where AngularJS shines the brightest of all the JavaScript frameworks available. AngularJS is a solid foundation for building scalable applications that run well on desktops and a broad array of mobile devices, with few if any modifications needed for each platform.

A New and Better Way

AngularJS is a JavaScript MVC framework that cuts development time for both web applications and mobile applications that run on multiple device platforms. Figure 3-3 shows a diagram of an AngularJS application that uses business logic that's exposed through REST web services. The REST services can run anywhere and be written in any programming language. Two popular frameworks used to build REST services are the Spring framework, written in Java, and ExpressJS for Node.js.

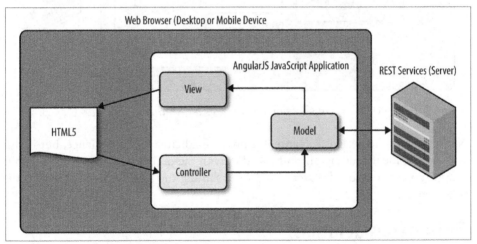

Figure 3-3. AngularJS application design

If you look closely at Figure 3-3, you can see that the entire AngularJS application runs on the user's hardware, in the user's web browser. That may be a desktop browser or the browser of a mobile device. With this design we shift the display logic from the server to the user's hardware, resulting in a much better user experience. The application runs faster and is much more responsive—more like a thick-client or native application than a browser-based application.

AngularJS applications harness the power of the user's hardware. The approach that's taken frees the server or servers to handle nothing but business logic and data access. Using REST services that send and receive JSON helps to greatly simplify AngularJS applications: JSON is a data-interchange format for REST services that is easy to read and understand.

Figure 3-4 shows the same AngularJS application deployed as part of an Android application. The JavaScript, CSS3, and HTML5 code is all the same regardless of where the application is deployed. If the application was designed from a mobile-first perspective, it should look great and run well on any platform.

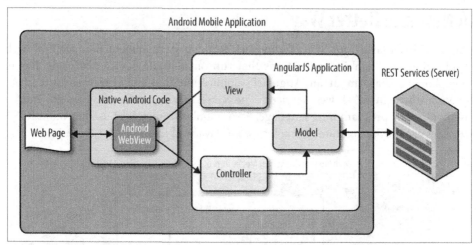

Figure 3-4. The AngularJS application deployed as an Android app

Not only does the design in Figure 3-4 produce a better user experience, but it also cuts development time significantly. And as with the design in Figure 3-3, the application runs entirely on the user's hardware, shifting the load from the server to the user's device.

Testing Considerations

We covered some of the basics of testing AngularJS applications back in Chapter 2. The ability to effectively and easily test AngularJS applications is one of the strongest motivators for using the framework. Not only are AngularJS applications faster to write, but they are also much faster and easier to test than conventional web framework–based applications. Here is why.

Test scripts for AngularJS, known as *test specifications*, are always written in Java-Script. There are no complex test frameworks to install like you find with traditional web frameworks. One more thing: JavaScript tests run faster than tests written for conventional web frameworks. That is very important when a continuous integration system is used.

Test execution speeds may not seem like a serious concern at first. But consider the continuous integration platforms like Travis CI and Jenkins that we discussed back in Chapter 2. If you had a small shop with five or six developers, test script execution speeds wouldn't usually be a concern. If you had a large enterprise shop, however, with a few hundred developers all running CI builds at the same time, then concerns would change quickly.

The two most popular test frameworks used for client-side JavaScript and AngularJS, Karma and Protractor, run on the Node.js framework. Applications and test scripts that run on Node.js run extremely fast. That is one of the major advantages of using Node.js. Continuous integration systems also use Node.js for JavaScript builds and to run test scripts. It is easy to see, then, why JavaScript testing is faster in a CI environment.

Responsive Design Considerations

Another consideration when you are comparing traditional web frameworks to AngularJS is how well responsive design is accomplished. A strong responsive design looks good both on a desktop and on all mobile devices that use the software. While you can build responsive applications with traditional web frameworks, it's not often done. Unfortunately, many web application developers often target desktops and maybe tablets and ignore the various smaller devices that use their websites.

Take, for example, the CSS3 code shown next. The code is taken from a server-side application written with CakePHP, a web MVC framework:

```
/* chapter3 server-side css3 */
/* not built for mobile */

.page-container{
  float: left;
  margin: 3% 0 0 0;
  padding: 0 0 0 0;
  width: 100%;
}
img {
  max-width: 50%;
}
.partner-form{
  float: left;
  width: 50%;
  margin: 0 0 0 25%;
  padding: 1% 5% 1% 5%;
  border-radius:7px;
  -moz-border-radius:7px; /* Firefox 3.6 and earlier */
  border: #230fba solid 1px;
}
.new-article-upload-wrapper{
```

```css
    float: left;
    width: 30%;
    margin: 0 0 0 35%;
    padding: 1%;
    border-radius:7px;
    -moz-border-radius:7px; /* Firefox 3.6 and earlier */
    border: #230fba solid 1px;
}
.login-title{
    float: left;
    width: 100%;
    margin: 6% 0 1% 0;
    text-align: center;
    font-size: 18pt;
    font-weight: bold;
}
.config-form-wrapper{
    float: left;
    width: 60%;
    padding: 0 0 0 0;
    margin: 0 0 0 20%;
    border-radius:7px;
    -moz-border-radius:7px; /* Firefox 3.6 and earlier */
    border: #230fba solid 1px;

}
.comment-form-wrapper{
    float: left;
    width: 60%;
    padding: 0 0 0 0;
    margin: 0 0 0 20%;
    border-radius:7px;
    -moz-border-radius:7px; /* Firefox 3.6 and earlier */
    border: #230fba solid 1px;

}
.summary-cell{
    height: 300px;
}

.summary-cell-data{
    height: 250px;
    font-size: 12pt;
}
```

An application styled with this code would look fine on a desktop, and maybe a tablet. There would be major styling issues with a small mobile device, however. A mobile wrapper application like the one I mentioned earlier that wrapped a website that used this code would be at a great disadvantage. You could never make the application look good on a small phone.

The code that follows is taken from a mobile application built with AngularJS. Notice the media query lines like @media screen and (min-width: 1200px) that wrap parts of the CSS3. Media queries let developers style AngularJS applications to specific screen sizes:

```
/* chapter3 mobile css3 */
/* built for mobile */

@media screen and (min-width: 1200px){
  .page-container{
    margin: 3% 0 0 0;
    padding: 0 0 0 0;
    width: 100%;
  }
  img {
    max-width: 50%;
  }
  .partner-form{
    width: 50%;
    margin: 0 0 0 25%;
    padding: 1% 5% 1% 5%;
    border-radius:7px;
    -moz-border-radius:7px; /* Firefox 3.6 and earlier */
  }
  .new-article-upload-wrapper{
    width: 30%;
    margin: 0 0 0 35%;
    padding: 1%;
    border-radius:7px;
    -moz-border-radius:7px; /* Firefox 3.6 and earlier */
  }
  .login-title{
    width: 100%;
    margin: 6% 0 1% 0;
    font-size: 18pt;
  }
  .config-form-wrapper{
    width: 60%;
    padding: 0 0 0 0;
    margin: 0 0 0 20%;
    border-radius:7px;
    -moz-border-radius:7px; /* Firefox 3.6 and earlier */
  }
  .comment-form-wrapper{
    width: 60%;
    padding: 0 0 0 0;
    margin: 0 0 0 20%;
    border-radius:7px;
    -moz-border-radius:7px; /* Firefox 3.6 and earlier */
  }
    .summary-cell{
        height: 300px;
```

```
    }
    .summary-cell-data{
        height: 250px;
        font-size: 12pt;
    }
}
@media screen and (max-width: 1200px){
    .page-container{
        margin: 5%  0 0 0;
        padding: 0 0 0 0;
        width: 100%;
    }
    img {
        max-width: 60%;
    }
    .nav-ds{
        margin: 0 0 0 0;
    }
    .nav-ds li{
        width: 11%;

    }
    .nav-ds li a{
        margin: 0 0 0 0;
        padding: 4% 0 4% 0;
    }
    .partner-form{
        width: 50%;
        margin: 0 0 0 25%;
        padding: 1% 5% 1% 5%;
        border-radius:7px;
        -moz-border-radius:7px; /* Firefox 3.6 and earlier */
    }
    .new-article-upload-wrapper{
        margin: 0 0 0 30%;
        padding: 1%;
        border-radius:7px;
        -moz-border-radius:7px; /* Firefox 3.6 and earlier */
    }
    .login-title{
        width: 100%;
        margin: 6% 0 1% 0;
        font-size: 18pt;
    }
    .config-form-wrapper{
        width: 60%;
        padding: 0 0 0 0;
        margin: 0 0 0 20%;
        border-radius:7px;
        -moz-border-radius:7px; /* Firefox 3.6 and earlier */
    }
    .comment-form-wrapper{
```

```css
            width: 60%;
            padding: 0 0 0 0;
            margin: 0 0 0 20%;
            border-radius:7px;
            -moz-border-radius:7px; /* Firefox 3.6 and earlier */
        }
        .summary-cell{
            height: 300px;
        }
        .summary-cell-data{
            height: 250px;
            font-size: 12pt;
        }
    }
@media screen and (max-width: 800px){
    .page-container{
        margin: 7%  0 0 0;
        padding: 0 0 0 0;
        width: 100%;
    }
    img {
        max-width: 70%;
    }
    .nav-ds{
        margin: 0 0 0 0;
    }
    .nav-ds li{
        width: 11%;

    }
    .nav-ds li a{
        margin: 0 0 0 0;
        padding: 4% 0 4% 0;
    }

    .partner-form{
        width: 60%;
        margin: 0 0 0 20%;
        padding: 1% 5% 1% 5%;
        border-radius:7px;
        -moz-border-radius:7px; /* Firefox 3.6 and earlier */
    }
    .new-article-upload-wrapper{
        width: 50%;
        margin: 0 0 0 25%;
        padding: 1%;
        border-radius:7px;
        -moz-border-radius:7px; /* Firefox 3.6 and earlier */
    }
    .login-title{
        width: 100%;
        margin: 6% 0 1% 0;
```

```css
        font-size: 16pt;
    }
    .config-form-wrapper{
        width: 80%;
        padding: 0 0 0 0;
        margin: 0 0 0 10%;
        border-radius:7px;
        -moz-border-radius:7px; /* Firefox 3.6 and earlier */
    }
    .comment-form-wrapper{
        width: 80%;
        padding: 0 0 0 0;
        margin: 0 0 0 10%;
        border-radius:7px;
    }
    .summary-cell{
        height: 300px;
    }
    .summary-cell-data{
        height: 250px;
        font-size: 10pt;
    }
}
@media screen and (max-width: 450px){
    .page-container{
        margin: 12%  0 0 0;
        padding: 0 0 0 0;
        width: 100%;
    }
    img {
        max-width: 100%;
    }
    .nav-ds{
        margin: 0 0 0 0;
    }
    .nav-ds li{
        width: 15%;

    }
    .nav-ds li a{
        margin: 0 0 0 0;
        padding: 4% 0 4% 0;
    }
    .partner-form{
        width: 100%;
        margin: 0 0 0 0%;
        padding: 1% 5% 1% 5%;
        border-radius:7px;
        -moz-border-radius:7px; /* Firefox 3.6 and earlier */
    }
    .new-article-upload-wrapper{
        width: 100%;
```

```
        margin: 0 0 0 0%;
        padding: 1%;
        border-radius:7px;
        -moz-border-radius:7px; /* Firefox 3.6 and earlier */
    }
    .login-title{
        width: 100%;
        margin: 6% 0 1% 0;
        font-size: 14pt;
    }
    .config-form-wrapper{
        width: 100%;
        padding: 0 0 0 0;
        margin: 0 0 0 0;
        border-radius:7px;
        -moz-border-radius:7px; /* Firefox 3.6 and earlier */
    }
    .comment-form-wrapper{
        float: left;
        width: 100%;
        padding: 0 0 0 0;
        margin: 0 0 0 0;
        border-radius:7px;
        -moz-border-radius:7px; /* Firefox 3.6 and earlier */
    }
    .summary-cell{
        height: 150px;
    }
    .summary-cell-data{
        height: 120px;
        font-size: 6pt;
    }
}
```

If the web application shown previously had been written with AngularJS, it would have been a simple task to convert the AngularJS application into a mobile application. The development team could then have fixed the CSS3 issues and been done. The application written with CakePHP had to be completely rewritten, however.

Conclusion

In this chapter we compared AngularJS applications to applications built with conventional server-side web frameworks. We identified many of the shortcomings of conventional server-side frameworks, especially as they relate to mobile applications, and gained an understanding of the serious limitations they pose on how developers build mobile applications.

We also looked at the many advantages of building applications with AngularJS, such as shorter development times and increased application speed and testability. We saw how AngularJS greatly simplifies the process of building responsive mobile applications, then looked at a real-world situation where a simple issue like poorly written CSS posed a serious problem for a mobile development team working with an application built using a conventional server-side web framework.

The information presented in this chapter is a great foundation for the material covered in the following chapters. We will now take our understanding of the advantages of AngularJS to the next level, exploring how AngularJS helps to simplify the process of interacting with backend systems using REST services.

Although this is not a book on REST services, we will cover the basics of REST services in Chapter 6, looking in detail at how AngularJS connects to these services and how to interface with JSON payloads. Chapter 7 will provide you with information on public REST service endpoints written especially for this book that you can use to complete the chapter exercises.

The REST services that you will use in Chapter 7 are built with ExpressJS, run on Node.js, and use JSON as the data-interchange format. The services used in that and other chapters are deployed to the cloud and open to anyone using this book as a learning tool. Before we get into all of that, however, we're going to take a look at AngularJS controllers.

AngularJS Controllers

AngularJS controllers are at the center of AngularJS applications and are probably the most important component to understand. Controllers are not always clearly defined in some JavaScript client-side frameworks, and that tends to confuse developers who have experience with MVC frameworks. That is not the case with AngularJS. AngularJS clearly defines controllers, and controllers are at the center of AngularJS applications.

Almost everything that happens in an AngularJS application passes through a controller at some point. Dependency injection is used to add the needed dependencies, as shown in the following example file, which illustrates how to create a new controller:

```
/* chapter4/controllers.js - a new controller */

var addonsControllers =
  angular.module('addonsControllers', []);

addonsControllers.controller('AddonsCtrl',
  ['$scope', 'checkCreds', '$location', 'AddonsList', '$http', 'getToken',
    function AddonsCtrl($scope, checkCreds, $location, AddonsList,
      $http, getToken) {
        if (checkCreds() !== true) {
            $location.path('/loginForm');
        }

        $http.defaults.headers.common['Authorization'] =
          'Basic ' + getToken();
        AddonsList.getList({},
            function success(response) {
                console.log("Success:" +
                    JSON.stringify(response));
                    $scope.addonsList = response;
```

```
        },
        function error(errorResponse) {
           console.log("Error:" +
                 JSON.stringify(errorResponse));
        }
      );
      $scope.addonsActiveClass = "active";
  }]);
```

In this code, we first create a new module named `addonsController` by making a call to the `module` method of `angular`. On the second line, we create a new controller named `AddonsCtrl` by calling the `controller` method of the `addonsControllers` module. Doing that attaches the new controller to that module. All controllers created in the *controllers.js* file will be added to the `addonsControllers` module.

Also notice the line `console.log("Success:" + JSON.stringify(response))`. Most modern browsers have accompanying developer tools that give developers easy access to the JavaScript console. This line uses the `JSON.stringify` method to log the JSON that's returned from the web service to the JavaScript console. Developers can easily use the JavaScript console to troubleshoot REST service issues by viewing the JSON logged in the `success` callback function, or in the `error` callback function if a service call fails.

Most developer tools and some IDEs, like NetBeans, also include JavaScript debuggers that allow developers to place breakpoints in both the `success` and `error` callback functions. Doing so allows the developer to take a fine-grained approach to troubleshooting REST services. Quite often, the developer can resolve otherwise complex REST service issues very quickly by using a JavaScript debugger.

The following code is an excerpt of the previous file. It shows how we use dependency injection to add dependencies to the new controller. This code shows `$scope`, `check Creds`, `$location`, `AddonsList`, `$http`, and `getTokens` as dependencies for the new controller. We have already covered the `$scope` briefly. For now it's not important what the other dependencies actually represent; you only need to understand they are required by the new controller:

```
/* chapter4/controllers.js excerpt */
/* using dependency injection */

['$scope', 'checkCreds', '$location', 'AddonsList', '$http', 'getToken',
   function AddonsCtrl($scope, checkCreds, $location, AddonsList,
     $http, getToken) {
}
```

This controller plays a major role in the application in which it was defined. Controllers really have two primary responsibilities in an application. We will take a look at those responsibilities in more detail in the next section.

Initializing the Model with Controllers

AngularJS controllers have two primary duties in an application. First, controllers should be used to initialize the model scope properties. When a controller is created and attached to the DOM, a child scope is created. The child scope holds a model used specifically for the controller to which it is attached. You can access the child scope by using the $scope object.

Create a copy of the Chapter 2 project and name it *AngularJsHelloWorld_chapter4*. We will use this new project for the rest of this chapter. You can also download the project from the GitHub project site (*https://github.com/KenWilliamson*).

Model properties can be added to the scope, and once added they are available inside the view templates. The controller code shown here illustrates how to add two properties to the scope. After adding the customer name and customer number to the scope, both are available to the view and can be accessed with double curly braces:

```
/* chapter4/controllers.js excerpt */

helloWorldControllers.controller('CustomerCtrl', ['$scope',
function CustomerCtrl($scope) {
    $scope.customerName = "Bob's Burgers";
    $scope.customerNumber = "44522";
}]);
```

Now add the new controller, CustomerCtrl, to your project's *controllers.js* file. We will make several additions to the *controllers.js* file in this chapter.

The following view template code shows how to access the newly added model properties inside the view template. All properties that need to be accessed from the view should be added to the $scope object:

```
<!-- chapter4/partials/customer.html -->

<div><b>Customer Name:</b> {{customerName}}</div>
<div><b>Customer Number:</b> {{customerNumber}}</div>
```

Now add a new HTML file under the *partials* folder and name it *customer.html*. Replace the generated code with the code just shown.

Adding Behavior with Controllers

The second primary use for controllers is adding behavior to the $scope object. We add behavior by adding methods to the scope, as shown in the following controller code. Here, we attach a changeCustomer method to $scope so that it can be invoked from inside the view. By doing this, we are adding behavior that allows us to change the customer name and customer number:

```
/* chapter4/controllers.js excerpt */

helloWorldControllers.controller('CustomerCtrl', ['$scope',
function CustomerCtrl($scope) {

    $scope.customerName = "Bob's Burgers";
    $scope.customerNumber = 44522;

    // add method to scope
    $scope.changeCustomer = function(){
      $scope.customerName = $scope.cName;
      $scope.customerNumber = $scope.cNumber;
    };

}]);
```

Add the changeCustomer method shown here to the CustomerCtrl controller defined in your *controllers.js* file.

The following code shows the *customer.html* file and the changes needed in the view to make use of the new behavior that was just added. We add two new properties to the model by using ng-model="cName" and ng-model="cNumber". We use ng-click="changeCustomer();" to invoke the new changeCustomer method that is attached to the scope:

```
<!-- chapter4/partials/customer.html -->

<div><b>Customer Name:</b> {{customerName}}</div>
<div><b>Customer Number:</b> {{customerNumber}}</div>

<form>

  <div>
    <input type="text" ng-model="cName" required/>
  </div>

  <div>
    <input type="number" ng-model="cNumber" required/>
  </div>

  <div>
    <button ng-click="changeCustomer();" >Change Customer</button>
  </div>

</form>
```

Modify the *customer.html* file to include the new form defined here.

Once the changeCustomer method is invoked, the new properties are attached to $scope and available to the controller. As you can see, we simply assign the two new properties bound to the model back to the original two properties, `customerName` and `customerNumber`, inside the `changeCustomer` method. Both `ng-model` and `ng-click` are AngularJS directives. We will cover directives in detail in Chapter 9.

Controller Business Logic

Controllers are used as just demonstrated to add business logic to an application. Business logic added in the controller, however, should be specific to the view associated with that one controller and used to support some display logic functionality of that one view. Any business logic that can be pushed off the client-side application should be implemented as a REST service and not actually inside the AngularJS application.

There is one caveat to this concept, however: REST services must have a response time of two (2) seconds or less. Long-running services will only cause delays in the UI and make for a bad user experience. Meeting the two-seconds-or-less rule requires having REST services that are properly designed and running on a backend system that scales well to load demand changes. There are other concerns related to mobile applications, but we will cover those in Chapter 7 and Chapter 8.

Business logic that can't be placed in REST services but needs to be available to multiple controllers should not be placed in the controller but should instead be placed in AngularJS non-REST services. In Chapter 8, we will cover business logic services in more detail. Business logic that is placed in the controller should be simple logic that relates only to the controller in which it is defined. Placing too much business logic inside an AngularJS application would be a bad design decision, however.

Presentation Logic and Formatting Data

Presentation logic should not be placed inside the controller but instead should be placed in the view. AngularJS has many features for DOM manipulation that help you avoid placing presentation logic in the controllers. The controller is also not the place where you should format data. AngularJS has features especially designed for formatting data, and that's where data formatting should take place. Some of those features will be covered in detail in the next chapter.

Form Submission

Now we will look at how form submissions are handled in AngularJS using controllers. The following code for the *newCustomer.html* file shows the view for a new form. Create a new HTML file under the *partials* folder and replace the generated code with the code listed here:

```
<!-- chapter4/partials/newCustomer.html -->

<form ng-submit="submit()" ng-controller="AddCustomerCtrl">

  <div>
    <input type="text" ng-model="cName" required/>
  </div>

  <div>
    <input type="text" ng-model="cCity" required/>
  </div>

  <div>
    <button type="submit" >Add Customer</button>
  </div>

</form>
```

As you can see, we use standard HTML for the form with nothing really special except the directives. The directive ng-submit binds the method named submit, defined in the AddCustomerCtrl controller, to the form for form submission. The ng-model directive binds the two input elements to scope properties.

Two or more controllers can be applied to the same element, and we can use control ler as to identify each individual controller. The following code shows how control ler as is used. You can see that addCust identifies the AddCustomerCtrl controller. We use addCust to access the properties and methods of the controller, as shown:

```
<!-- chapter4/partials/newCustomer.html (with controller as) -->

<form ng-submit="addCust.submit()"
      ng-controller="AddCustomerCtrl as addCust">

  <div>
    <input type="text" ng-model="addCust.cName" required/>
  </div>

  <div>
    <input type="text" ng-model="addCust.cCity" required/>
  </div>

  <div>
    <button id="f1" type="submit" >Add Customer</button>
  </div>

</form>
```

The following code shows the AddCustomerCtrl controller and how we use it to handle the submitted form data. Here we use the path method on the AngularJS service $location to change the path after the form is submitted. The new path is *http://*

localhost:8383/AngularJsHelloWorld_chapter4/index.html#!/addedCustomer/name/city.

Add this code to the *controllers.js* file:

```
/* chapter4/controllers.js */

helloWorldControllers.controller('AddCustomerCtrl',
['$scope', '$location',
  function AddCustomerCtrl($scope, $location) {
    $scope.submit = function(){
      $location.path('/addedCustomer/' + $scope.cName + "/" + $scope.cCity);
    };
}]);
```

That's all that is needed to handle the form substitution process. We will now look at how we get access to the submitted values inside another controller.

Using Submitted Form Data

The *app.js* file shown next includes the new route definitions. Modify the *app.js* file in the Chapter 3 project and add the new routes. Make sure your file looks like the file shown here:

```
/* chapter4/app.js */
/* App Module */

var helloWorldApp = angular.module('helloWorldApp', [
    'ngRoute',
    'helloWorldControllers'
]);

helloWorldApp.config(['$routeProvider', '$locationProvider',
function($routeProvider, $locationProvider) {
  $routeProvider.
  when('/', {
    templateUrl: 'partials/main.html',
    controller: 'MainCtrl'
  }).when('/show', {
    templateUrl: 'partials/show.html',
    controller: 'ShowCtrl'
  }).when('/customer', {
    templateUrl: 'partials/customer.html',
    controller: 'CustomerCtrl'
  }).when('/addCustomer', {
    templateUrl: 'partials/newCustomer.html',
    controller: 'AddCustomerCtrl'
  }).when('/addedCustomer/:customer/:city', {
    templateUrl: 'partials/addedCustomer.html',
    controller: 'AddedCustomerCtrl'
  });
```

```
$locationProvider.html5Mode(false).hashPrefix('!');
}]);
```

You can see there are two path parameters, `customer` and `city`, for the `addedCusto`
`mer` route. The values are passed as arguments to a new controller, `AddedCusto`
`merCtrl`, shown in the following excerpt. We use the `$routeParams` service in the new
controller to get access to the values passed as path parameter arguments in the URL.
By using `$routeParams.customer` we get access to the customer name, and `$route`
`Params.city` gets us access to the city:

```
/* chapter4/controllers.js excerpt */

helloWorldControllers.controller('AddedCustomerCtrl',
['$scope', '$routeParams',
function AddedCustomerCtrl($scope, $routeParams) {

    $scope.customerName = $routeParams.customer;
    $scope.customerCity = $routeParams.city;

}]);
```

Add the new controller, `AddedCustomerCtrl`, to your *controllers.js* file now.

The code for our new `addedCustomer` template is shown next. Once again, we use
AngularJS double curly braces to get access to and display both the `customerName`
and `customerCity` properties in the view:

```
<!-- chapter4/addedCustomer.html -->

<div><b>Customer Name: </b> {{customerName}}</div>

<div><b>Customer City: </b> {{customerCity}}</div>
```

To add the template to the project, create a new HTML file in the *partials* folder and
name it *addedCustomer.html*. Replace the generated code with the code just shown.
Note how simple it is to submit forms with AngularJS. Simplicity is one of the factors
that makes AngularJS a great choice for any JavaScript client-side application project.

JS Test Driver

The rest of this chapter will cover setting up a test environment and testing AngularJS
controllers. NetBeans has a great testing environment for both JS Test Driver and
Karma. We will focus first on setting up JS Test Driver for unit testing. We will then
take a look at Karma for unit testing. To begin, do the following:

1. Download (*http://bit.ly/js-test-driver*) the JS Test Driver JAR.

2. In the Services tab, right-click "JS Test Driver" and click "Configure" (see Figure 4-1).

3. Select the location of the JS Test Driver JAR just downloaded and choose the browser of your choice (see Figure 4-2).

4. Right-click the project node, then click "New"→"Other"→"Unit Tests."

5. Select "jsTestDriver Configuration File" and click "Next."

6. Make sure the file is placed in the *config* subfolder, as shown in Figure 4-3.

7. Make sure the checkbox for "Download and setup Jasmine" is checked.

8. Click "Finish."

9. Right-click the project node, click Properties, and select "JavaScript Testing."

10. Select "jsTestDriver" from the drop-down box.

Figure 4-1. Right-click "JS Test Driver" in the Services tab

Figure 4-2. Select your browser(s)

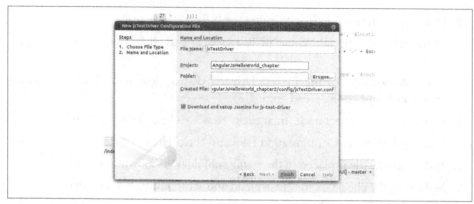

Figure 4-3. Make sure the file is created in the config subfolder

The following code shows the JS Test Driver configuration file. Inside the file, we specify the server URL that is used by JS Test Driver. We also specify the needed library files in the `load` section of the file, along with the locations of our JavaScript files and test scripts:

```
/*  chapter4/jsTestdriver.conf */

server: http://localhost:42442
load:
- test/lib/jasmine/jasmine.js
- test/lib/jasmine-jstd-adapter/JasmineAdapter.js

- public_html/js/libs/angular.min.js
- public_html/js/libs/angular-mocks.js
- public_html/js/libs/angular-cookies.min.js
- public_html/js/libs/angular-resource.min.js
- public_html/js/libs/angular-route.min.js
- public_html/js/*.js

- test/unit/*.js
exclude:
```

Notice we've added *angular-mocks.js* to the list of required AngularJS library files. That file is needed for unit testing AngularJS applications. So, before continuing, add the *angular-mocks.js* file to the *js/libs* folder.

Creating Test Scripts

Next, create a new JavaScript file in the *unit* subfolder of the newly created *Unit Test* folder, as shown in Figure 4-4. Name the new file *controllerSpec.js*.

Figure 4-4. Create the controllerSpec.js file in the unit subfolder

The contents of the *controllerSpec.js* file are shown next. Our test script filename will end with *Spec*. The file specifies a standard set of unit tests commonly used to test AngularJS controllers. Notice that we have a test for each of our controllers defined in the *controllers.js* file:

```
/* chapter4/controllerSpec.js */

/* Jasmine specs for controllers go here */
describe('Hello World', function() {

  beforeEach(module('helloWorldApp'));

  describe('MainCtrl', function(){
    var scope, ctrl;
    beforeEach(inject(function($rootScope, $controller) {
      scope = $rootScope.$new();
      ctrl = $controller('MainCtrl', {$scope: scope});
    }));

    it('should create initialed message', function() {
      expect(scope.message).toEqual("Hello World");
    });

  });

  describe('ShowCtrl', function(){
    var scope, ctrl;

    beforeEach(inject(function($rootScope, $controller) {
      scope = $rootScope.$new();
      ctrl = $controller('ShowCtrl', {$scope: scope});
    }));

    it('should create initialed message', function() {
      expect(scope.message).toEqual("Show The World");
```

```
    });

  });

  describe('CustomerCtrl', function(){
    var scope, ctrl;

    beforeEach(inject(function($rootScope, $controller) {
      scope = $rootScope.$new();
      ctrl = $controller('CustomerCtrl', {$scope: scope});
    }));

    it('should create initialed message', function() {
      expect(scope.customerName).toEqual("Bob's Burgers");
    });
  });
});
```

This test script uses Jasmine as the behavior-driven development framework for testing our code. We will use Jasmine for all our test scripts in this book.

Here is the complete *controllers.js* file:

```
/* chapter4/controllers.js */

'use strict';
/* Controllers */
var helloWorldControllers =
  angular.module('helloWorldControllers', []);

helloWorldControllers.controller('MainCtrl', ['$scope',
  function MainCtrl($scope) {
    $scope.message = "Hello World";
}]);

helloWorldControllers.controller('ShowCtrl', ['$scope',
  function ShowCtrl($scope) {
    $scope.message = "Show The World";
}]);

helloWorldControllers.controller('CustomerCtrl', ['$scope',
  function CustomerCtrl($scope) {
    $scope.customerName = "Bob's Burgers";
    $scope.customerNumber = 44522;
    $scope.changeCustomer = function(){
    $scope.customerName = $scope.cName;
    $scope.customerNumber = $scope.cNumber;
  };
}]);

helloWorldControllers.controller('AddCustomerCtrl',
['$scope', '$location',
  function AddCustomerCtrl($scope, $location) {
```

```
        $scope.submit = function(){
            $location.path('/addedCustomer/' + $scope.cName + "/" + $scope.cCity);
        };
}]);

helloWorldControllers.controller('AddedCustomerCtrl',
['$scope', '$routeParams',
    function AddedCustomerCtrl($scope, $routeParams) {
        $scope.customerName = $routeParams.customer;
        $scope.customerCity = $routeParams.city;
}]);
```

 To save time, you can download the Chapter 4 code from GitHub (*http://bit.ly/lajs-github*). For a complete guide to JavaScript testing in NetBeans, see the documentation at on the NetBeans website (*http://bit.ly/nb-debug*).

Testing with JS Test Driver

Now to actually test the controllers we've defined, just right-click the project node and select "Test" from the menu. If your project is configured correctly, you should see a success message for all three controllers that were tested. If you have any issues with the test results, go back over the configuration files and validate that all your files match those listed in this chapter. If you continue to have problems, download and run the source code from the project site (*https://github.com/KenWilliamson*).

Testing with Karma

Karma is a new and fun way to unit test AngularJS applications. We will use Karma here to test the controllers that we tested earlier.

Installing Karma

Karma runs on Node.js, as mentioned in Chapter 2, so first you must install Node.js if it's not already installed. Refer to *nodejs.org* for installation details for your particular operating system. You'll also need to install the Node.js package manager (npm) on your system. npm is a command-line tool used to add the needed Node.js modules to a project.

Now, in the root of the Chapter 4 project, create a JSON file named *package.json* and add the following content. The *package.json* file is used as a configuration file for Node.js:

```
{
    "name": "package.json",
    "devDependencies": {
        "karma": "*",
```

```
            "karma-chrome-launcher": "*",
            "karma-firefox-launcher": "*",
            "karma-jasmine": "*",
            "karma-junit-reporter": "*",
            "karma-coverage": "*"
        }
    }
```

Open a command-line window on your system, and navigate to the root of the Chapter 4 project. You should see the *package.json* file when you list out the files in the folder.

Type this command to actually install the Node.js dependencies defined in the *package.json* file:

```
npm install
```

Now install the Karma command-line interface (*karma-cli*) by typing the following command:

```
npm install -g karma-cli
```

 Make sure to record the location where *karma-cli* was installed. You will need the location later in this chapter.

This command installs the command-line tool globally on your system.

All the Node.js dependencies specified in the *package.json* file will be installed under the *node_modules* folder inside the project root folder. If you list out the files and folders, you should see the new folder. You won't be able to see the new folder inside NetBeans, however.

Karma Configuration

Next, create a new Karma configuration file named *karma.conf.js* inside the project test folder. Do the following:

1. Right-click the project in NetBeans.
2. Select "New"→"Other"→"Unit Tests."
3. Create a new Karma configuration file inside the test folder.

Edit the new *karma.conf.js* file and add the following code:

```
/* chapter4/karma.conf.js */
```

```
module.exports = function (config) {
    config.set({
        basePath: '../',
        files: [
            "public_html/js/libs/angular.min.js",
            "public_html/js/libs/angular-mocks.js",
            "public_html/js/libs/angular-route.min.js",
            "public_html/js/*.js",
            "test/**/*Spec.js"
        ],
        exclude: [
        ],
        autoWatch: true,
        frameworks: [
            "jasmine"
        ],
        browsers: [
            "Chrome",
            "Firefox"
        ],
        plugins: [
            "karma-junit-reporter",
            "karma-chrome-launcher",
            "karma-firefox-launcher",
            "karma-jasmine"
        ]
    });
};
```

Now do the following to set Karma as the test framework:

1. Right-click the project.

2. Select "Properties."

3. Select "JavaScript Testing" from the list of categories.

4. Select "Karma" as the testing provider.

5. Select the location of the *karma-cli* tool installed earlier.

6. Select the location of the *karma.conf.js* file just created.

7. Select "OK."

Running Karma Unit Tests

Now to actually run the unit tests (using the test specification written earlier) under Karma, right-click the project and select "Test" from the menu. Karma will start. You should see both Chrome and Firefox browser windows open. The NetBeans test results window should open and display three passed tests for Chrome and three passed tests for Firefox.

If you get any error messages or failed tests, go back over this section and verify that you completed all the configurations and installations. You can also download the Chapter 4 code from the GitHub project site (*https://github.com/KenWilliamson*).

End-to-End Testing with Protractor

Protractor is a new test framework for running end-to-end (E2E) tests. Protractor lets you run tests that exercise the application as a user would. With Protractor E2E testing, you can test various pages, navigate through each page from within the test script, and find any potential defects. Protractor also integrates with most continuous integration build systems.

Installing Protractor

Like Karma, Protractor is a Node.js-based test framework. The Protractor team recommends installing Protractor globally. To do so, open a command-line window and type the command:

```
npm install -g protractor
```

Protractor relies on WebDriverJS, so we will also use this command to update WebDriverJS with the latest libraries:

```
webdriver-manager update
```

Configuring Protractor

Next, we will create a Protractor configuration file for our project. Create a new Java-Script file named *conf.js* under the *test* folder of the Chapter 4 project. Enter the code shown here in the new file:

```
/ *chapter4/conf.js */

exports.config = {
  seleniumAddress: 'http://localhost:4444/wd/hub',
  specs: ['e2e/Hw-spec.js']
};
```

Creating Protractor Test Specifications

Now we need to create a Protractor test specification. Do the following:

1. Create a new folder under the *test* folder of the project and name it *e2e*.

2. Create a new JavaScript file inside the new *e2e* folder and name it *Hw-spec.js*.

Now copy the code shown here into the new *Hw-spec.js* file:

```
/* chapter4/Hw-spec.js Protractor test specification */

describe("Hello World Test", function(){
    it("should test the main page", function(){
        browser.get(
          "http://localhost:8383/AngularJsHelloWorld_chapter4/");
        expect(browser.getTitle()).toEqual("AngularJS Hello World");

        var msg = element(by.binding("message")).getText();
        expect(msg).toEqual("Hello World");

        browser.get(
        "http://localhost:8383/AngularJsHelloWorld_chapter4/#!/show");
        expect(browser.getTitle()).toEqual("AngularJS Hello World");

        var msg = element(by.binding("message")).getText();
        expect(msg).toEqual("Show The World");

        browser.get(
      "http://localhost:8383/AngularJsHelloWorld_chapter4/#!/
addCustomer");

        element(by.model("cName")).sendKeys("tester");
        element(by.model("cCity")).sendKeys("Atlanta");
        element(by.id("f1")).click();

        browser.get(
      "http://localhost:8383/
AngularJsHelloWorld_chapter4/#!/addedCustomer/tester/Atlanta");

        var msg = element(by.binding("customerName")).getText();
        expect(msg).toEqual("Customer Name: tester");

        var msg = element(by.binding("customerCity")).getText();
        expect(msg).toEqual("Customer City: Atlanta");
    });
});
```

Starting the Selenium Server

WebDriverJS runs on the Selenium Server. To start the Selenium Server that runs
Protractor tests (using the *webdriver-manager* tool), open a new command window
and enter the following command:

```
webdriver-manager start
```

Running Protractor

Now that the Selenium Server is running, we can run our Protractor tests. Open a
new command window, navigate to the root of the Chapter 4 project, and type this
command:

```
protractor test/conf.js
```

You should see a browser window open. You should then see the test script navigate through the pages of the Chapter 4 application. If you watch the browser window closely, you will see the script enter values in the form that adds a new customer. When the Protractor script has finished, the browser window will close.

You should see results like the following in the command window when the Protractor script completes. The number of seconds that it takes the script to finish will vary depending on your particular system:

```
Finished in 3.368 seconds
1 test, 6 assertions, 0 failures
```

 For more information on testing with Protractor, see the project site on GitHub (*http://angular.github.io/protractor*). Protractor has a complete set of documentation to help you get started.

Conclusion

Unit testing AngularJS controllers allows us to validate the basic functionality of each controller. For now, our tests are very simple. Testing a controller that retrieves data from a REST service, for example, would be a more complex task.

End-to-end testing is a bit more involved, and can be designed to completely exercise the entire application. For now, our E2E tests are also simple. E2E tests help to identify software defects early in the development process when used with CI build systems.

We'll be doing more testing in the next chapter, where we focus on AngularJS views.

AngularJS Views and Bootstrap

We will now start a new AngularJS blog project that uses public REST services created especially for this book. We will work on the blog project for the rest of this book. You can also download the project code from GitHub (*http://bit.ly/lajs-github*). We will start off by building the views and the controllers for those views.

Twitter Bootstrap is a free collection of HTML and CSS templates. We will build the AngularJS views with the help of Twitter Bootstrap to help cut development time. Once we have the views and controllers in place and understand their operation, we will focus on the model and REST services (in the next two chapters).

AngularJS Templates

AngularJS views are defined by building templates (partials). Views in AngularJS are composed of HTML code with directives added, such as the `ng-model` directive shown previously. AngularJS builds the views dynamically at runtime by merging the templates with the properties passed to the templates in the `$scope` object. The end result is pure HTML code bound to the `ng-view` directive, as explained back in Chapter 1. We will cover the `ng-view` directive again in this chapter as a review.

Creating the Blog Project

Start a new HTML5 project in NetBeans and call it *AngularJsBlog*. Set up the folder structure as shown in Figure 5-1. Move the downloaded AngularJS, jQuery, and Bootstrap library files to the *js/libs* folder, as shown.

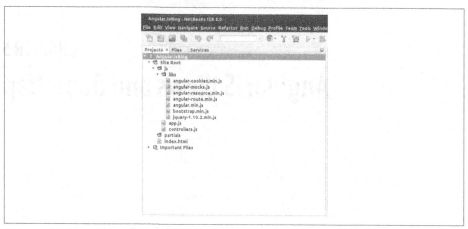

Figure 5-1. Blog project folder structure

We'll begin with the code for the *index.html* file. As you can see, we load the needed library files with the <script> tag in the <head> section of the page. The tag <div ng-view></div> is where all dynamic content is inserted. As the user clicks on links in the application, existing content attached to the tag is removed and new dynamic content is then attached to that same tag:

```
<!-- chapter5/index.html -->

<!DOCTYPE html>
<html lang="en" ng-app="blogApp">

<head>
<title>AngularJS Blog</title>

<meta name="viewport" content="width=device-width, initial-scale=1.0">
<meta http-equiv="Content-Type" content="text/html; charset=UTF-8">

<script src="js/libs/jquery-1.10.2.min.js"></script>
<script src="js/libs/angular.min.js"></script>
<script src="js/libs/angular-route.min.js"></script>
<script src="js/libs/angular-resource.min.js"></script>
<script src="js/libs/angular-cookies.min.js"></script>
<script src="js/app.js"></script>
<script src="js/controllers.js"></script>

</head>
<body>

<div ng-view></div>

</body>
</html>
```

Adding a New Blog Controller

Next we will set up the controllers for our new blog application. The following code defines the blogControllers module and the BlogCtrl controller for that module. We will define more controllers on the blogControllers module as we work on the blog application. For now, the *controllers.js* file is relatively small:

```
/* chapter5/controllers.js */

'use strict';
/* Controllers */

var blogControllers =
  angular.module('blogControllers', []);

blogControllers.controller('BlogCtrl', ['$scope',
function BlogCtrl($scope) {

  $scope.blogArticle =
    "This is a blog post about AngularJS.
    We will cover how to build a blog and how to add
    comments to the blog post.";
}]);
```

Next is the code for the *app.js* file that starts the booting process for the blog application. This is where we define the route for the main page of the blog. As you can see, we define ngRoute and blogControllers as dependencies of the application at startup time, using inline array annotations. The two dependencies are injected into the application using DI and are available throughout the application when we need them. Any controllers attached to the blogControllers module are accessible to the blogApp module (the AngularJS application):

```
/* chapter5/app.js */

'use strict';
/* App Module */

var blogApp = angular.module('blogApp', [
  'ngRoute',
  'blogControllers'
]);

blogApp.config(['$routeProvider', '$locationProvider',
  function($routeProvider, $locationProvider) {
    $routeProvider.
      when('/', {
        templateUrl: 'partials/main.html',
        controller: 'BlogCtrl'
    });
```

```
$locationProvider.html5Mode(false).hashPrefix('!');
}]);
```

The routes are defined in the application configuration block. For now, we will only define the main page of the blog. We define `BlogCtrl` as the controller and `'parti als/main.html'` as the template used for the main route. We will add more routes as we need them.

Adding a New Blog Template

Now we will add a simple template file and test run the application before adding code to the template. Right-click the NetBeans project folder and add a new HTML page named *main.html* in the *partials* folder. Replace the generated HTML code with the code shown here:

```
<!-- chapter5/main.html -->

{{blogArticle}}
```

Right-click the project folder and select "Run" from the menu. If you set up the project correctly, the browser should open with the following text displayed: "This is a blog post about AngularJS. We will cover how to build a blog and how to add comments to the blog post." This tells us our application is properly configured. Now we will use Twitter Bootstrap and HTML to build a menu and main page for our blog.

Twitter Bootstrap

You should have already added *bootstrap.min.js* to the project. If you run into JavaScript errors related to Twitter Bootstrap, you can easily replace the *bootstrap.min.js* file with the nonminified *bootstrap.js* file distributed by Twitter. Using the nonminified version of the file allows the developer to place breakpoints in the Bootstrap JavaScript file and debug any related issues. We will only cover the basics of Twitter Bootstrap here. For more documentation and tutorials on Bootstrap, see the project site (*http://getbootstrap.com/getting-started*).

First, we need to add three more folders and some additional Twitter Bootstrap files to the project. We will add all the Bootstrap files here, although much of Bootstrap is not actually used in this project. Do the following:

1. Add a subfolder named *css* under the *Site Root* folder.
2. Add a subfolder named *fonts* under the *Site Root* folder.
3. Add a subfolder named *lib-css* under the *Site Root* folder.
4. Copy the *bootstrap-theme.min.css* and *bootstrap.min.css* files into the *lib-css* folder.

5. Copy the following files to the *fonts* folder:
   a. *glyphicons-halflings-regular.eot*

   b. *glyphicons-halflings-regular.svg*

   c. *glyphicons-halflings-regular.ttf*

   d. *glyphicons-halflings-regular.woff*

6. Add the two lines of code shown next to the *index.html* file. These two lines are all that we need to make use of Twitter Bootstrap:

```
<!-- chapter5/index.html excerpt -->

<link rel="stylesheet" href="lib-css/bootstrap.min.css" media="screen"/>

<script src="js/libs/bootstrap.min.js"></script>
```

Here is the completed *index.html* file:

```
<!-- chapter5/index.html complete file -->

<!DOCTYPE html>
<html lang="en" ng-app="blogApp">

<head>
<title>Blog</title>

<meta name="viewport" content="width=device-width, initial-scale=1.0">
<meta http-equiv="Content-Type" content="text/html; charset=UTF-8">

<link rel="stylesheet" href="lib-css/bootstrap.min.css" media="screen"/>
<script src="js/libs/bootstrap.min.js"></script>
<script src="js/libs/jquery-1.10.2.min.js"></script>
<script src="js/libs/angular.min.js"></script>
<script src="js/libs/angular-route.min.js"></script>
<script src="js/libs/angular-resource.min.js"></script>
<script src="js/libs/angular-cookies.min.js"></script>
<script src="js/app.js"></script>
<script src="js/controllers.js"></script>

</head>

<body>
<div ng-view></div>
</body>

</html>
```

Figure 5-2 shows the project file structure. Make sure your project is set up as shown. The added CSS files and fonts will give us access to many time-saving features of Twitter Bootstrap. We will now add a Bootstrap menu to our project.

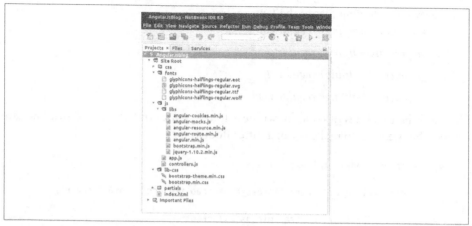

Figure 5-2. The completed file structure for the blog project

Adding a Bootstrap Menu

The following are the contents of the *menu.html* file. Most of the code shown is clearly explained on the Bootstrap project site (*http://getbootstrap.com/getting-started/*). The styles added to the menu here are defined in the *bootstrap.min.css* file added in the previous section. If you have questions on Bootstrap menus, please refer to the Bootstrap project documentation for a fuller explanation. Your *menu.html* file should look like this:

```
<!-- chapter5/menu.html -->

<nav class="navbar navbar-inverse navbar-fixed-top" role="navigation">

<!-- Brand and toggle get grouped for better mobile display -->
<div class="container">
<div class="navbar-header">
<button type="button" class="navbar-toggle" data-toggle="collapse"
  data-target=".navbar-collapse">
<span class="sr-only">Toggle navigation</span>
<span class="icon-bar"></span>
<span class="icon-bar"></span>
<span class="icon-bar"></span>
</button>
<a class="navbar-brand" style="{{brandColor}}" href="#!/">Angular Blog</a>
</div>

<!-- Collect the nav links, forms, and other content for toggling -->
<div class="collapse navbar-collapse">

<ul class="nav navbar-nav">
<li class="{{aboutActiveClass}}"><a href="#!about">About</a></li>
<li class="">
```

```
<a href="https://github.com/KenWilliamson">Download Project Code</a></li>
</ul>

</div><!-- /.navbar-collapse -->

</div>
</nav>
```

Here's how to add the *menu.html* file inside the *main.html* file:

```
<!-- chapter5/main.html -->

<div ng-include src="'partials/menu.html'"></div>

{{blogArticle}}
```

The first line shows the needed addition to *main.html*. As you see, we use the ng-include directive to include the menu template inside the main template. This approach allows us to keep the menu completely separate from the other templates. Using this approach makes the code base easy to maintain and understand. We will now focus on using other Bootstrap styles to enhance our blog.

Adding Mock Blog Data

We will modify the BlogCtrl controller and set a list of blog posts as a scope property named blogList. The modified *controllers.js* code is shown here. The JSON list represents the data that will eventually be retrieved from a REST service. For now, however, we will just hardcode the JSON into the controller as mock data. There are more advanced ways to add mock data to an AngularJS application, but that is beyond the scope of this book. Let's take a look at the controllers file:

```
/* chapter5/controllers.js */

'use strict';
/* Controllers */
var blogControllers =
  angular.module('blogControllers', []);

blogControllers.controller('BlogCtrl', ['$scope',
  function BlogCtrl($scope) {
    $scope.blogList = [
      {
        "_id": 1,
        "date": 1400623623107,
        "introText": "This is a blog post about AngularJS.
          We will cover how to build",
        "blogText": "This is a blog post about AngularJS.
          We will cover how to build a blog and how to add
          comments to the blog post."
      },
```

```
    {
      "_id": 2,
      "date": 1400267723107,
      "introText": "In this blog post we will learn how to
        build applications based on REST",
      "blogText": "In this blog post we will learn how to
        build applications based on REST web services that
        contain most of the business logic needed for the
        application."
    }
  ];
}]);
```

As you can see, there is no presentation logic in this code, and no data formatting is
done in the controller. The date, for instance, is sent to the view as a long value that is
a standard representation of a date in most programming languages. Trying to format
the date in the controller would be an incorrect design that shouldn't be used. AngularJS has many features that make formatting and presenting data easy; we'll look at
some of these next.

Using CSS3 to Style the Page

Now we will add some CSS3 to style our pages. Do the following:

1. Right-click the project node and create a new CSS file named *style.css*.

2. Place the following code into the new CSS file:

```
/* chapter5/styles.css */

body{
  font-family: arial;
  font-size: 12pt;
  color: #2a6496;
}

.post-wrapper{
  float: left;
  width: 100%;
  margin: 5% 0 0 0;
  padding: 0 0 0 0;
}

.blog-post-label{
  float: left;
  width: 100%;
  margin: 10% 0 0 0;
  padding: 0 0 0 0;
  text-align: center;
  font-weight: bold;
  font-size: 16pt;
```

```
}

.blog-post-outer{
  float: left;
  width: 60%;
  margin: 2% 0 2% 20%;
  padding: 1%;
  background: #e0e0e0;
  border-radius:6px;
  -moz-border-radius:6px; /* Firefox 3.6 and earlier */
  border: darkgreen solid 1px;
}

.blog-intro-text{
  float: left;
  width: 100%;
  margin: 0 0 0 0;
  padding: 0 0 0 0;
  text-align: center;
}

.blog-read-more{
  float: left;
  width: 100%;
  margin: 2% 0 0 0;
  padding: 0 0 0 0;
  text-align: center;
}
```

Now modify the *index.html* file, adding the line shown here to load the newly created CSS file:

```
<!-- chapter5/index.html excerpt -->

<link rel="stylesheet" href="css/styles.css" media="screen"/>
```

The complete *index.html* file is shown here. Make sure your version of the file matches this one:

```
<!-- chapter5/index.html complete file -->

<!DOCTYPE html>
<html lang="en" ng-app="blogApp">

<head>
<title>Blog</title>

<meta name="viewport" content="width=device-width, initial-scale=1.0">
<meta http-equiv="Content-Type" content="text/html; charset=UTF-8">
<link rel="stylesheet" href="lib-css/bootstrap.min.css" media="screen"/>

<script src="js/libs/jquery-1.10.2.min.js"></script>
<script src="js/libs/bootstrap.min.js"></script>
```

```
<script src="js/libs/angular.min.js"></script>
<script src="js/libs/angular-route.min.js"></script>
<script src="js/libs/angular-resource.min.js"></script>
<script src="js/libs/angular-cookies.min.js"></script>

<link rel="stylesheet" href="css/styles.css" media="screen"/>

<script src="js/app.js"></script>
<script src="js/controllers.js"></script>
</head>

<body>
<div ng-view></div>
</body>

</html>
```

Adding Styles and Presentation Logic

You must modify the *main.html* template to make use of the new styles and to add proper presentation logic for displaying blog posts and formatting data. Modify your *main.html* to match the code shown here. The second line, `<div id="container" class="container">`, sets up a Bootstrap container and is standard practice with Twitter Bootstrap:

```
<!-- chapter5/main.html -->

<div ng-include src="'partials/menu.html'"></div>

<div id="container" class="container">

<div class="blog-post-label">Blog Posts</div>
<div class="post-wrapper">
<div ng-repeat="blogPost in blogList">
<div class="blog-post-outer">

<div class="blog-intro-text">
Posted: {{blogPost.date | date:'MM/dd/yyyy @ h:mma'}}
</div>

<div class="blog-intro-text">
{{blogPost.introText}}
</div>

<div class="blog-read-more">
<a href="#!blogPost/{{blogPost._id}}">Read More</a>
</div>

</div>
</div>
```

```
  </div>
  </div>
```

The Bootstrap container handles much of the page styling for various screen sizes to make the page responsive for any screen size on any device. Inside the container we use the CSS that was added in the *styles.css* file. We won't focus much on the custom CSS, because it is not specific to AngularJS and is covered in many other books on Cascading Style Sheets.

We will, however, take a look at the AngularJS directives that allow us to build the presentation logic in the view and handle formatting. The line `<div ng-repeat="blogPost in blogList">` is very important to understanding AngularJS views. The directive `ng-repeat` works like a `for` loop, iterating over the list of blog posts in the scope property `blogList`.

Each iteration through the list gives access to each item in the list through the variable `blogPost`. We use the line `{{blogPost.introText}}` to display the intro text (the value of the `introText` property of the `blogPost` variable).

Another line that is very important is the HTML template binding `{{blogPost.date | date:'MM/dd/yyyy @ h:mma'}}`, which allows us to format the date in the view, where it should be formatted. As I stated previously, there are many features of AngularJS for formatting data, and this is just one. As you can see, the template code is simple and easy to understand.

We will now add a controller, route, and view to display the individual blog post when a user clicks on the "View More" link. If you look closely, you can see that the link passes `blogPost.id` as a path parameter argument to a new route, */blogPost*. We will now add the needed code to view a blog post.

Viewing the Blog Post

To add the extra functionality, first append this CSS code to the end of the *styles.css* file:

```
/* chapter5/styles.css excerpt */

.blog-entry-wrapper{
  float: left;
  width: 100%;
  margin: 1% 0 0 0;
  padding: 0 0 0 0;
}

.blog-entry-outer{
  float: left;
  width: 60%;
  margin: 2% 0 2% 20%;
```

```
    padding: 1%;
    background: #e0e0e0;
    border-radius:6px;
    -moz-border-radius:6px; /* Firefox 3.6 and earlier */
    border: darkgreen solid 1px;
  }

.blog-comment-wrapper{
  float: left;
  width: 50%;an HTML5 project
  margin: 2% 0 2% 25%;
  padding: 1%;
  border-radius:6px;
  -moz-border-radius:6px; /* Firefox 3.6 and earlier */
  border: darkgreen solid 1px;
}

.blog-entry-comments{
  float: left;
  width: 96%;
  margin: 2% 0 2% 2%;
  padding: 1%;
  background: #f5e79e;
  border-radius:6px;
  -moz-border-radius:6px; /* Firefox 3.6 and earlier */
  border: darkgreen solid 1px;
}

.blog-comment-label{
  float: left;
  width: 100%;
  margin: 1% 0 0 0;
  padding: 0 0 0 0;
  text-align: center;
  font-weight: bold;
  font-size: 16pt;
}
```

Then add this code to the bottom of the *controllers.js* file:

```
/* chapter5/controllers.js excerpt */

blogControllers.controller('BlogViewCtrl',
  ['$scope', '$routeParams',
    function BlogViewCtrl($scope, $routeParams) {

      var blogId = $routeParams.id;
      var blog1 = {
        "_id": 1,
        "date": 1400623623107,
        "introText": "This is a blog post about AngularJS.
          We will cover how to build",
```

```
          "blogText": "This is a blog post about AngularJS.
            We will cover how to build a blog and how to add
            comments to the blog post.",
          "comments" :[
            {
              "commentText" : "Very good post. I love it."
            },
            {
              "commentText" : "When can we learn services."
            }
          ]
      };

    var blog2 = {
      "_id": 2,
      "date": 1400267723107,
      "introText": "In this blog post we will learn how to
        build applications based on REST",
      "blogText": "In this blog post we will learn how to
        build applications based on REST web services that
        contain most of the business logic needed for the application.",
      "comments" :[
        {
          "commentText" : "REST is great. I want to know more."
        },
        {
          "commentText" : "Will we use Node.js for REST services?."
        }
      ]
    };

    if(blogId === '1'){
      $scope.blogEntry = blog1;
    }else if(blogId === '2'){
      $scope.blogEntry = blog2;
    }


}]);
```

Next, add a new template file named *blogPost.html* in the *partials* folder and replace
the generated code with the code shown here:

```
<!-- chapter5/blogPost.html -->

<div ng-include src="'partials/menu.html'"></div>

<div id="container" class="container">

<div class="blog-post-label">Blog Entry</div>
<div class="blog-entry-wrapper">

<div class="blog-intro-text">
```

```
Posted: {{blogEntry.date| date:'MM/dd/yyyy @ h:mma'}}
</div>

<div class="blog-entry-outer">
{{blogEntry.blogText}}
</div>

<div class="blog-comment-wrapper">
<div class="blog-comment-label">Blog Comments</div>
<div class="blog-entry-comments" ng-repeat="comment in
blogEntry.comments">
{{comment.commentText}}
</div>

</div>
</div>
</div>
```

And add this code to the route provider section of *app.js*:

```
/* chapter5/app.js excerpt */

.when('/blogPost/:id', {
templateUrl: 'partials/blogPost.html',
controller: 'BlogViewCtrl'
```

The complete route definition is shown here:

```
/* chapter5/app.js excerpt - complete route */

blogApp.config(['$routeProvider', '$locationProvider',
function($routeProvider, $locationProvider) {

  $routeProvider.
    when('/', {
      templateUrl: 'partials/main.html',
      controller: 'BlogCtrl'
    }).when('/blogPost/:id', {
      templateUrl: 'partials/blogPost.html',
      controller: 'BlogViewCtrl'
  });

  $locationProvider.html5Mode(false).hashPrefix('!');
}]);
```

As you can see, the effort required to add a new page was minimal. If you look at the route definition, you'll see the id passed as a path parameter argument. Look at the new controller and you can see how we handle the id parameter. Since we do not yet have REST services in place, we hardcoded the JSON for the two blog posts into the controller.

Once we retrieve the passed id from $routeParams, we use that to determine which blog entry to set as a scope property. Notice that we never actually set a scope property until we know which blog entry gets sent to the view. Notice also that blog1 and blog2 are defined as local variables. Only the variables needed in the page are set as scope properties.

You should never add properties to the scope that are not needed in the view.

Running the Blog Application

Now let's run the project to test our work. Right-click the project node and select "Run" from the menu. If you made all the changes correctly, you should see the screen shown in Figure 5-3. If you get a different result, go back over the changes in this chapter and verify that you made all the needed modifications.

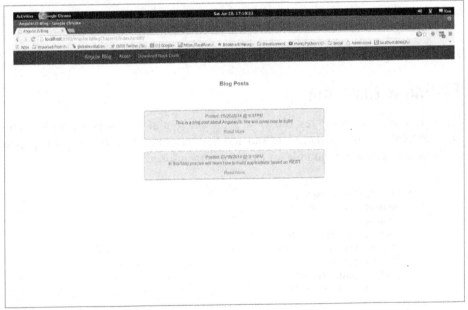

Figure 5-3. Successful result from running the project

If you have problems that you can't resolve, download the project code from GitHub (*http://bit.ly/lajs-github*) and run that code. Once the project is running, click the "Read More" link on the first blog post. You should then see the screen shown in

Figure 5-4. Click the "Read More" link on the second blog post, and you should see a similar page.

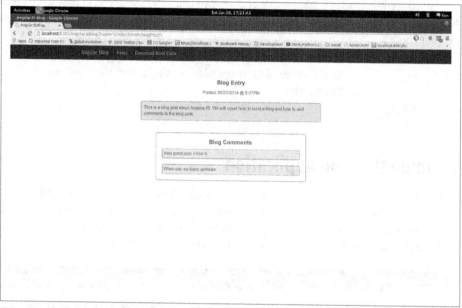

Figure 5-4. Viewing the comments on the first blog post

Testing with Karma

We will use Karma now to test our view. From the root of the Chapter 5 project, create a JSON file named *package.json* and add the following contents. The *package.json* file is used as a configuration file for Node.js, as mentioned in Chapter 4:

```
{
    "name": "package.json",
    "devDependencies": {
        "karma": "*",
        "karma-chrome-launcher": "*",
        "karma-firefox-launcher": "*",
        "karma-jasmine": "*",
        "karma-junit-reporter": "*",
        "karma-coverage": "*"
    }
}
```

Open a command-line window on your system, and navigate to the root of the Chapter 5 project. You should see the *package.json* file when you list out the files in the folder. Now type the following command to install the Node.js dependencies defined in the *package.json* file. This is the same process described in Chapter 4:

```
npm install
```

Karma Configuration

Now we will create a new Karma configuration file named *karma.conf.js* inside the project's *test* folder, as we did in Chapter 4. Do the following:

1. Right-click the project in NetBeans.
2. Select "New"→"Other"→"Unit Tests."
3. Create a new Karma configuration file inside the *test* folder.

Edit the new *karma.conf.js* file and add the code shown here:

```
/* chapter5/karma.conf.js */

module.exports = function (config) {
    config.set({
        basePath: '../',
        files: [
            "public_html/js/libs/angular.min.js",
            "public_html/js/libs/angular-mocks.js",
            "public_html/js/libs/angular-route.min.js",
            "public_html/js/*.js",
            "test/**/*Spec.js"
        ],
        exclude: [
        ],
        autoWatch: true,
        frameworks: [
            "jasmine"
        ],
        browsers: [
            "Chrome",
            "Firefox"
        ],
        plugins: [
            "karma-junit-reporter",
            "karma-chrome-launcher",
            "karma-firefox-launcher",
            "karma-jasmine"
        ]
    });
};
```

Now do the following to configure Karma as the test framework:

1. Right-click the project.
2. Select "Properties."
3. Select "JavaScript Testing" from the list of categories.

4. Select "Karma" as the testing provider.

5. Select the location of the *karma-cli* tool installed in Chapter 4.

6. Select the location of the *karma.conf.js* file just created, and select "OK."

Karma Test Specifications

Now we need to add new test specifications for the Chapter 5 project. Do the following:

1. Create a new folder named *unit* under the *test* folder of the project.

2. Create a new JavaScript file named *controllerSpec.js* under the *unit* folder.

3. Enter the code shown here in the new file:

```
/* chapter5/controllerSpec.js */

describe('AngularJS Blog Application', function () {

    beforeEach(module('blogApp'));

    describe('BlogCtrl', function () {
        var scope, ctrl;

        beforeEach(inject(function ($rootScope, $controller) {

            scope = $rootScope.$new();
            ctrl = $controller('BlogCtrl', {$scope: scope});
        }));

        it('should create show blog entry count', function () {
            console.log("blogList:" + scope.blogList.length);
            expect(scope.blogList.length).toEqual(2);
        });
    });

    describe('BlogViewCtrl', function () {
        var scope, ctrl, $httpBackend;

        beforeEach(inject(function (_$httpBackend_,
            $routeParams, $rootScope, $controller) {
            $httpBackend = _$httpBackend_;
            $httpBackend.expectGET('blogPost').respond({_id: '1'});

            $routeParams.id = '1';

            scope = $rootScope.$new();

            ctrl = $controller('BlogViewCtrl', {$scope: scope});
        }));
```

```
        it('should show blog entry id', function () {
            expect(scope.blogEntry._id).toEqual(1);
        });
    });
});
```

Karma Testing

The new test specification will unit test both controllers. Right-click the project and select "Test" from the menu. Karma will start. You should see both Chrome and Firefox browser windows open. The NetBeans test results window should open and display two passed tests for Chrome and two passed tests for Firefox.

If you get any error messages or failed tests, go back over this section and verify that you completed all the configurations and installations. You can also download the Chapter 5 code from the GitHub project site (*https://github.com/KenWilliamson*).

End-to-End Testing

Next, we need to create a Protractor configuration file for the project. Create a new JavaScript file named *conf.js* under the *test* folder of the Chapter 5 project. Enter the code shown here in the new file:

```
/* chapter5/conf.js Protractor configuration file */

exports.config = {
  seleniumAddress: 'http://localhost:4444/wd/hub',
  specs: ['e2e/blog-spec.js']
};
```

Protractor Test Specification

Now we need to create a Protractor test specification. Do the following:

1. Create a new folder under the *test* folder of the project and name it *e2e*.

2. Create a new JavaScript file inside the new *e2e* folder and name it *blog-spec.js*.

Then copy the code shown next into the new *blog-spec.js* file.

 Make sure the lines browser.get("http://localhost:8383/Angu larJsBlog/"); match the URL that you use on your system to call the blog application. The URL can be different for different development environments and can depend on how you named your project.

```
/* chapter5/blog-spec.js */

describe("Blog Application Test", function(){
    it("should test the main blog page", function(){

        browser.get("http://localhost:8383/AngularJsBlog/");
        expect(browser.getTitle()).toEqual("AngularJS Blog");

        //gets the blog list
        var blogList = element.all(by.repeater('blogPost in blogList'));

        //tests the size of the blogList
        expect(blogList.count()).toEqual(2);
        browser.get(
        "http://localhost:8383/AngularJsBlog/#!/blogPost/1");
        expect(browser.getTitle()).toEqual("AngularJS Blog");

        //gets the comment list
        var commentList = element.all(
         by.repeater('comment in blogEntry.comments'));

        //checks the size of the commentList
        expect(commentList.count()).toEqual(2);
    });
});
```

Protractor Testing

Start a new command window and enter the following command to start the test server:

```
webdriver-manager start
```

Open a new command window and navigate to the root of the Chapter 5 project. Type the command:

```
protractor test/conf.js
```

You should see a browser window open. You should then see the test script navigate through the pages of the blog application. When the Protractor script has finished, the browser window will close.

You should see results like the following in the command window when the Protractor script completes. The number of seconds that it takes the script to finish will vary depending on your particular system:

```
Finished in 1.377 seconds
1 test, 4 assertions, 0 failures
```

Conclusion

In this chapter we built our view using Twitter Bootstrap. We also made our application responsive to different screen sizes using CSS3. We configured both Karma and Protractor for our blog project, and ran both unit and end-to-end tests.

We will now cover REST services and how they are used in AngularJS. Then we will move on to the model.

AngularJS and REST Services

In the new era of mobile everywhere, the business logic for AngularJS applications should always be placed in REST services whenever possible. AngularJS applications should be kept clean and simple. Why? As AngularJS evolves over the next few years, it is very possible that most AngularJS applications will be rewritten.

This means that any business logic placed inside an AngularJS application will need to be rewritten as well—a serious consideration for applications containing large amounts of business logic. REST services, on the other hand, may be around for years to come. As web services technologies evolve, many REST services may undergo upgrades and modifications, but a complete service rewrite is unlikely in most cases. The best place for business logic is the place that will undergo the least amount of change and be available to all types of applications, now and in the future.

REST Services

REST (REpresentational State Transfer) services allow for a "separation of concerns." REST services are not concerned with the user interface or user state, and clients that use REST services are not concerned with data storage or business logic. Clients can be developed independently of the REST services, as we have shown in previous chapters, using mock data. REST services can likewise be developed independently of the client, with no concern for client specifics or even the types of clients using the services. REST services should perform in the same way for all clients.

REST services should be stateless. A REST service should never hold data in a session variable. All information needed for a REST service call should be contained in the request and header passed from the client to the service. Any state should be held in the client and not in the service. There are many ways to hold state in an AngularJS application, including local storage, cookies, or cache storage.

A REST web service is said to be RESTful when it adheres to the following constraints:

- It's URL-based (e.g., *http://www.micbutton.com/rs/blogPost*).
- It uses an Internet media type such as JSON for data interchange.
- It uses standard HTTP methods (GET, PUT, POST, DELETE).

HTTP methods have a particular purpose when used with REST services. The following is the standard way that HTTP methods should be used with REST services:

1. POST should be used to:
   a. Create a new resources.
   b. Retrieve a list of resources when a large amount of request data is required to be passed to the service.
2. PUT should be used to update a resource.
3. GET should be used to retrieve a resource or a list of resources.
4. DELETE should be used to delete a resource.

For example, the following would be the proper use of HTTP methods:

1. POST: `http://www.micbutton.com/rs/blogPost` to create a new blog post
2. PUT: `http://www.micbutton.com/rs/blogPost` to update a blog post
3. GET: `http://www.micbutton.com/rs/blogPost/50` to get the blog post with `id` equal to 50
4. DELETE: `http://www.micbutton.com/rs/blogPost/50` to delete the blog post with `id` equal to 50

AngularJS and REST Services

AngularJS REST service calls are asynchronous Ajax calls based on the `$q` service's promise and deferred APIs. We will not cover promises, deferred objects, or Ajax in this book. If you do not understand how Ajax is used to make asynchronous calls, now would be a good time to research these topics. Making asynchronous Ajax REST service calls is not specific to AngularJS or any other client-side JavaScript framework. Many libraries provide Ajax functionality, including jQuery, Dojo, and others.

Ways to Create AngularJS Services

There are three ways to create and register services in AngularJS. They are as follows:

- Using the `service` function

- Using the `provider` function
- Using the `factory` function

Here's how to create a service with the `service` function (we will not use this method to create services in this book):

```
/* chapter6/ service function */

var blogServices = angular.module('blogServices', ['ngResource']);
blogServices.service('BlogPost', [...]
```

You can also create services with the `provider` function, as shown here:

```
/* chapter6/ provider function */

var blogServices = angular.module('blogServices', ['ngResource']);
blogServices.provider('BlogPost', [...]
```

The third way to create services in AngularJS is with the `factory` function. This is the most commonly used method, and the method we will use to create AngularJS services throughout this book:

```
/* chapter6/ factory function */

var blogServices = angular.module('blogServices', ['ngResource']);
blogServices.factory('BlogPost', [...]
```

We will now look at how to connect to REST services in AngularJS, although we will not actually implement the service code in our blog application until Chapter 7. We need to get a good theoretical understanding of AngularJS services before we start coding. Once we have that understanding, we will be set for Chapter 7.

Ways to Communicate with REST Services

There are currently two ways to communicate with REST services using AngularJS:

The `$http` service
> This service provides low-level interaction with REST services using the browser's `XMLHttpRequest` object.

The `$resource` object
> This object provides a high-level approach to interacting with REST services, simplifying the process considerably.

We will focus mostly on using the `$resource` object for communicating with REST services and leave the `$http` service discussion to other books (although we will use the `$http` service in later chapters for handling Basic Authentication headers). All our project code uses the `$resource` object.

The following code shows how to define an AngularJS service that can be used to interact with the BlogPost REST service. Notice that we pass the REST service URL to the $resource object. The methods defined match the REST services that are defined on that particular URL. Once the BlogPost service is defined, it can be used like a standard JavaScript object to access the different REST services defined on this URL:

```
/* chapter6/services.js */

'use strict';
/* Services */

var blogServices =
 angular.module('blogServices', ['ngResource']);

blogServices.factory('BlogPost', ['$resource',
function($resource) {

return $resource("http://www.micbutton.com/rs/blogPost", {}, {
   get: {method: 'GET', cache: false, isArray: false},
   save: {method: 'POST', cache: false, isArray: false},
   update: {method: 'PUT', cache: false, isArray: false},
   delete: {method: 'DELETE', cache: false, isArray: false}
   });

}]);
```

Using the $resource object is by far the easiest way to call REST services. As you can see from this example, the AngularJS service code is straightforward and really fairly uncomplicated. Even when many services are defined, the *services.js* file is relatively simple.

The AngularJS $http service mentioned earlier is another way to call REST services. However, using the $http service would require many more lines of code related to REST service calls than we need using the $resource object. We do use the $http service in several places in the blog application, though, such as to send a Basic Authentication header to REST services. We will cover that in later chapters.

Updating the Project for REST

Before we can use our service, the new *services.js* file must be loaded at runtime and the new services module, blogServices, must be specified as a dependency of the application at startup time. Here is the line that should be added to the *index.html* file to load the *services.js* file:

```
/* chapter6/index.html excerpt */

<script src="js/services.js"></script>
```

And here is the complete *index.html* file, with this addition:

```
<!-- chapter6/index.html complete file -->

<!DOCTYPE html>
<html lang="en" ng-app="blogApp">

<head>
<title>AngularJS Blog</title>

<meta name="viewport" content="width=device-width, initial-scale=1.0">
<meta http-equiv="Content-Type" content="text/html; charset=UTF-8">


<link rel="stylesheet" href="lib-css/bootstrap.min.css" media="screen"/>
<link rel="stylesheet" href="css/styles.css" media="screen"/>


<script src="js/libs/jquery-1.10.2.min.js"></script>
<script src="js/libs/bootstrap.min.js"></script>
<script src="js/libs/angular.min.js"></script>
<script src="js/libs/angular-route.min.js"></script>
<script src="js/libs/angular-resource.min.js"></script>
<script src="js/libs/angular-cookies.min.js"></script>

<script src="js/app.js"></script>
<script src="js/controllers.js"></script>
<script src="js/services.js"></script>


</head>

<body>
<div ng-view></div>
</body>

</html>
```

The following code shows how we use inline annotations to add the new BlogServi
ces module as a dependency of the application at startup time. Once the new module
is added here, the services defined on the module can be used by any controller in the
application:

```
/* chapter6/app.js */

'use strict';
/* App Module */
```

```
var blogApp = angular.module('blogApp', [
  'ngRoute',
  'blogControllers',
  'blogServices'
]);


blogApp.config(['$routeProvider', '$locationProvider',
  function($routeProvider, $locationProvider) {
    $routeProvider.
      when('/', {
      templateUrl: 'partials/main.html',
      controller: 'BlogCtrl'
    }).when('/blogPost/:id', {
      templateUrl: 'partials/blogPost.html',
      controller: 'BlogViewCtrl'
    });

    $locationProvider.html5Mode(false).hashPrefix('!');
}]);
```

REST Services and Controllers

Now let's look at how to use the BlogPost service inside the BlogViewCtrl controller. First we must define the service as a requirement of the controller, as shown here. We then make a call to the get method and pass the id as an argument. We also define two callback functions, success and error (if you do not understand JavaScript callback functions, now would be a good time to stop and research how they work):

```
/* chapter6/controllers.js excerpt */

blogControllers.controller('BlogViewCtrl',
  ['$scope', '$routeParams', 'BlogPost',

  function BlogViewCtrl($scope, $routeParams, BlogPost) {
    var blogId = $routeParams.id;

    BlogPost.get({id: blogId},
      function success(response) {
      console.log("Success:" + JSON.stringify(response));
      $scope.blogEntry = response;
    },
      function error(errorResponse) {
        console.log("Error:" + JSON.stringify(errorResponse));
      }
    );
}]);
```

When a call is made to the `BlogViewCtrl` controller, the `id` is retrieved from `$route Params`. A call is then made to the `get` method of the `BlogPost` service, passing the `id` as an argument. At that point, the call to the controller completes.

Theoretically we don't know when the REST service call will return results, but when it does, either the `success` callback function or the `error` callback function will be called. If the REST service call fails, the code inside the `error` callback function should handle the error condition. If the REST service call is successful, the code inside the `success` callback function handles the success functionality.

The JSON Response

Now let's take a look at the JSON response object returned upon success. If the REST service call is successful, we set the JSON returned as the value of a scope property named `blogEntry`. The property is at that point bound to the view, and AngularJS updates the view with the new values that were retrieved from the REST service call. If the REST service call fails, the screen is not updated, but we log the error to the console to help diagnose the failure. The JSON response object returned from a successful call looks like this:

```
{ "chapter: 6,"JSON": "response"}

{
    "_id":1,
    "date":1400623623107,
    "introText":"This is a blog post about AngularJS.
      We will cover how to build",
    "blogText":"This is a blog post about AngularJS.
      We will cover how to build a blog and how to add
      comments to the blog post.",
    "comments":[
        {
            "commentText":"Very good post. I love it."
        },
        {
            "commentText":"When can we learn services."
        }
    ]
}
```

List Services

If we wanted a list of blog posts, we could define the following REST service: GET: `http://www.micbutton.com/rs/blogList`. Let's take a look at how we would define that service in the *services.js* file. Notice that we specify `isArray: true`. This defines the service as returning a list and not an individual resource:

```
/* chapter6/services.js excerpt */

blogServices.factory('BlogList', ['$resource',
function($resource) {
  return
$resource
("http://nodeblog-micbuttoncloud.rhcloud.com/NodeBlog/blogList",
{}, {
    get: {method: 'GET', cache: false, isArray: true}
  });

}]);
```

Following is the controller code used to access the BlogList service. We inject the service into the controller as we did earlier, and like before, we pass success and error callback functions to the service call. The response from a successful service call is assigned to the blogList property of the scope and passed to the view:

```
/* chapter6/controllers.js excerpt */

blogControllers.controller('BlogCtrl', ['$scope', 'BlogList',
    function BlogCtrl($scope, BlogList) {

    BlogList.get({},
      function success(response) {
        console.log("Success:" + JSON.stringify(response));
        $scope.blogList = response;
    },
      function error(errorResponse) {
        console.log("Error:" + JSON.stringify(errorResponse));
      }
    );
}]);
```

We access the JSON inside the view by using the blogList scope property, as shown here. This is the same technique we used in Chapter 5. We use the ng-repeat directive to iterate over the list as before:

```
<!-- chapter6/main.html excerpt -->

<div ng-repeat="blogPost in blogList">

<div class="blog-post-outer">
<div class="blog-intro-text">

Posted: {{blogPost.date | date:'MM/dd/yyyy @ h:mma'}} </div>
<div class="blog-intro-text"> {{blogPost.introText}} </div>

<div class="blog-read-more">

<a href="#!blogPost/{{blogPost._id}}">Read More</a>
```

```
</div>
```

Testing Services with Karma

The best way to test AngularJS services is with Karma. We used Karma as one of our test frameworks in previous chapters. Unit testing a service lets us validate that the unit of code that is used to build the service is working correctly. Unit testing an AngularJS service that connects to a REST service is a potential cause of errors, however.

REST service calls are asynchronous, so there can be a delay before the service call results are available to the part of the application that initiated the REST call. Considering that a REST service is not actually part of the unit of code that we would be testing with a unit test, we shouldn't be too concerned about REST calls when unit testing.

Karma, as I mentioned before, should be the unit test framework for our blog application. The following code shows how we modify a normal Karma configuration file to allow us to test code where the AngularJS $resource object is used. Notice the line "public_html/js/libs/angular-resource.min.js". With that line, we tell Karma to use the AngularJS *angular-resource.min.js* file. That file is needed only when we're working with code that calls REST services:

```
/* chapter6/karma.conf.js */

module.exports = function (config) {
    config.set({
        basePath: '../',
        files: [
            "public_html/js/libs/angular.min.js",
            "public_html/js/libs/angular-mocks.js",
            "public_html/js/libs/angular-route.min.js",
            "public_html/js/libs/angular-resource.min.js",
            "public_html/js/*.js",
            "test/**/*Spec.js"
        ],
        exclude: [
        ],
        autoWatch: true,
        frameworks: [
            "jasmine"
        ],
        browsers: [
            "Chrome",
            "Firefox"
        ],
        plugins: [
            "karma-junit-reporter",
```

```
            "karma-chrome-launcher",
            "karma-firefox-launcher",
            "karma-jasmine"
        ]
    });
};
```

Karma Service Specifications

In order to test AngularJS services, we need to add a test specification specifically for the blog application services. The following code shows a *servicesSpec.js* file. The test specification has unit testing for two services. The first unit test is for the BlogList service, and the second test is for the BlogPost service:

```
/* chapter6/servicesSpec.js */

describe('AngularJS Blog Service Testing', function () {

    describe('test BlogList', function () {
        var $rootScope;
        var blogList;

        beforeEach(module('blogServices'));

        beforeEach(inject(function ($injector) {
            $rootScope = $injector.get('$rootScope');
            blogList = $injector.get('BlogList');
        }));

        it('should test BlogList service', function () {
            expect(blogList).toBeDefined();
        });

    });

    describe('test BlogPost', function () {
        var $rootScope;
        var blogPost;

        beforeEach(module('blogServices'));

        beforeEach(inject(function ($injector) {
            $rootScope = $injector.get('$rootScope');
            blogPost = $injector.get('BlogPost');
        }));

        it('should test BlogPost service', function () {
            expect(blogPost).toBeDefined();
        });

    });
```

```
});
```

Notice in this code that we use `$injector` to inject the two services directly into the test scripts. As I mentioned earlier, we are not testing the REST services themselves; we are only testing the AngularJS services that connect to REST services. The tests should succeed even if the REST services are down for some reason.

End-to-End Testing

End-to-end testing done with Protractor is a much better way to test the functionality of REST services and the applications associated with them. Most modern software development teams use some type of continuous integration (CI) build system. Most CI systems can be configured to run end-to-end tests using Protractor.

Protractor E2E testing can even be configured to run tests against production environments. More often, however, E2E testing is written to run against services running on QA servers. E2E testing is a good way to test an application the same way a user would use the application.

Protractor Configuration

The following is a configuration file for Protractor. A specification file named *blog-spec.js* is referenced from the configuration file:

```
/* chapter6/conf.js Protractor configuration file */

exports.config = {
  seleniumAddress: 'http://localhost:4444/wd/hub',
  specs: ['e2e/blog-spec.js']
};
```

Protractor Test Specification

Let's take a look at the contents of the *blog-spec.js* file. You can see that the `browser.get(URL)` call can be made against any accessible URL. The URL could point to a local development box, a QA server, or a production server. REST services can be thoroughly tested with a Protractor test script:

```
/* chapter6/blog-spec.js Protractor test specification */

describe("Blog Application Test", function(){
    it("should test the main blog page", function(){

        browser.get(
          "http://localhost:8383/AngularJsBlogChapter6/");
        expect(browser.getTitle()).toEqual("AngularJS Blog");

        //gets the blog list
```

```
var blogList =
    element.all(by.repeater('blogPost in blogList'));

//tests the size of the blogList
expect(blogList.count()).toEqual(1);


browser.get(
    "http://localhost:8383/AngularJsBlogChapter6
     /#!/blogPost/5394e59c4f50850000e6b7ea");
expect(browser.getTitle()).toEqual("AngularJS Blog");

//gets the comment list
var commentList =
    element.all(by.repeater('comment in blogEntry.comments'));

//checks the size of the commentList
expect(commentList.count()).toEqual(2);
});
})
```

Conclusion

This concludes our discussion of REST service basics. Throughout the rest of this book we'll be working with live REST services. As we proceed, you will gain a better understanding of REST service concepts. We will now start working with actual REST services created especially for this book.

AngularJS Models

AngularJS models are held in the $scope object. In AngularJS, $scope is used to gain access to the model related to a particular controller. $rootScope is a parent scope that can be used to save and access model properties that span multiple controllers. The use of $rootScope is highly discouraged in most designs, however. There is only one $rootScope in an application. $scope is a child scope of $rootScope.

A properly designed AngularJS application will have little or no use for $rootScope to store model properties. In this chapter we will focus only on $scope, used to store the model retrieved from REST services.

Public REST Services

The REST services used for this chapter are available at *http://nodeblog-micbuttoncloud.rhcloud.com/NodeBlog*. The services are open to the public and written in JavaScript using Node.js, ExpressJS, and MongoDB. In Chapter 11, you will deploy the same REST services with your AngularJS blog application as a MEAN stack (MongoDB, ExpressJS, AngularJS, and Node.js) application. You will then deploy the MEAN stack to the cloud using a free RedHat OpenShift account.

The following excerpt shows how AngularJS services access the REST services used for this chapter. The REST services return the same JSON that was previously hard-coded in the controllers:

```
/* chapter7/services.js excerpt */

$resource(
  "http://nodeblog-micbuttoncloud.rhcloud.com/NodeBlog/blog/:id"
  ...
$resource(
```

```
"http://nodeblog-micbuttoncloud.rhcloud.com/NodeBlog/blogList"
...
```

The complete modified *services.js* file is shown here:

```
/* chapter7/services.js complete file */

'use strict';

/* Services */

var blogServices =
  angular.module('blogServices', ['ngResource']);

blogServices.factory('BlogPost', ['$resource',
  function($resource) {
    return $resource(
      "http://nodeblog-micbuttoncloud.rhcloud.com/NodeBlog/blog/:id",
    {}, {
      get: {method: 'GET', cache: false, isArray: false},
      save: {method: 'POST', cache: false, isArray: false},
      update: {method: 'PUT', cache: false, isArray: false},
      delete: {method: 'DELETE', cache: false, isArray: false}
    });
}]);


blogServices.factory('BlogList', ['$resource',
  function($resource) {
    return $resource(
      "http://nodeblog-micbuttoncloud.rhcloud.com/NodeBlog/blogList",
    {}, {
      get: {method: 'GET', cache: false, isArray: true}
    });
}]);
```

Changes to the Controllers

Shown next is the *controllers.js* file. The changes made here greatly simplify the controllers. The services needed for each individual controller are injected and made accessible for that particular controller to use. The blog ID is passed as a path parameter argument to the BlogPost service. A path parameter is used because we defined /id: at the end of the BlogPost service URL in the *services.js* file. If we removed the */:id* from the end of the service URL, AngularJS would pass the value as a query parameter argument instead. The updated file looks like this:

```
/* chapter7/controllers.js */

'use strict';
/* Controllers */
```

```
var blogControllers =
    angular.module('blogControllers', []);

blogControllers.controller('BlogCtrl',
  ['$scope', 'BlogList',
    function BlogCtrl($scope, BlogList) {
        $scope.blogList = [];
        BlogList.get({},
                function success(response) {
                    console.log("Success:" +
                       JSON.stringify(response));
                    $scope.blogList = response;

                },
                function error(errorResponse) {
                    console.log("Error:" +
                       JSON.stringify(errorResponse));
                }
        );
}]);

blogControllers.controller('BlogViewCtrl', ['$scope',
   '$routeParams', 'BlogPost',
     function BlogViewCtrl($scope, $routeParams, BlogPost) {
        var blogId = $routeParams.id;
        $scope.blg = 1;
        BlogPost.get({id: blogId},
                function success(response) {
                    console.log("Success:" +
                       JSON.stringify(response));
                    $scope.blogEntry = response;

                },
                function error(errorResponse) {
                    console.log("Error:" +
                       JSON.stringify(errorResponse));
                }
        );
}]);
```

Model Properties

Once you've added the JSON returned from the REST service to the model by assigning it to a scope property, that JSON is made available to the view. All scope properties are accessed from inside the view, as described in previous chapters. There are no changes that need to be made in the view.

If you have used other JavaScript client-side frameworks, by now you should see the simplicity of AngularJS models. With AngularJS, there are no model classes that need to be defined; you don't need to write model Ajax code or create model objects that have to be bound to the views. All you have to do is assign model properties to the scope. The AngularJS framework handles the rest.

AngularJS models greatly simplify the creation of JavaScript applications. You can cut what potentially could be thousands of lines of model-related code down to only a few lines. By cutting lines of code you also cut valuable development time, and potentially the number of developers needed on a project. The simplicity of the model code also makes applications easier to maintain or enhance, once again cutting costs by cutting development time.

Blog Application Public Services

Now we will make the needed changes to enable our blog application to use the public REST services discussed in the previous chapter. First, we must add the *services.js* file to our project.

Right-click the project and add a new JavaScript file named *services.js* under the *js* folder, as shown in Figure 7-1.

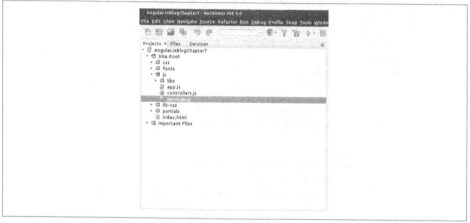

Figure 7-1. Adding the services.js file

Add this code to the newly created file:

```
/* chapter7/services.js */

'use strict';
/* Services */

var blogServices =
    angular.module('blogServices', ['ngResource']);

blogServices.factory('BlogPost', ['$resource',
    function($resource) {
```

```
    return $resource(
      "http://nodeblog-micbuttoncloud.rhcloud.com/NodeBlog/blog/:id",
   {}, {
      get: {method: 'GET', cache: false, isArray: false},
      save: {method: 'POST', cache: false, isArray: false},
      update: {method: 'PUT', cache: false, isArray: false},
      delete: {method: 'DELETE', cache: false, isArray: false}
   });
}]);

blogServices.factory('BlogList', ['$resource',
  function($resource) {
    return $resource(
      "http://nodeblog-micbuttoncloud.rhcloud.com/NodeBlog/blogList",
   {}, {
   get: {method: 'GET', cache: false, isArray: true}
   });
}]);
```

Now add the new *services.js* file to the *index.html* file's <head> section, as shown here, so the file can be loaded by our AngularJS application:

```
<!-- chapter7/index.html excerpt -->

<script src="js/services.js"></script>
```

Modifying the HTML

The complete *index.html* file is shown here for convenience:

```
<!-- chapter7/index.html -->

<!DOCTYPE html>
<html lang="en" ng-app="blogApp">
<head>
<title>AngularJS Blog</title>
<meta name="viewport" content="width=device-width, initial-scale=1.0">
<meta http-equiv="Content-Type" content="text/html; charset=UTF-8">

<link rel="stylesheet" href="lib-css/bootstrap.min.css" media="screen"/>
<link rel="stylesheet" href="css/styles.css" media="screen"/>

<script src="js/libs/jquery-1.10.2.min.js"></script>
<script src="js/libs/bootstrap.min.js"></script>
<script src="js/libs/angular.min.js"></script>
<script src="js/libs/angular-route.min.js"></script>
<script src="js/libs/angular-resource.min.js"></script>
<script src="js/libs/angular-cookies.min.js"></script>

<script src="js/app.js"></script>
<script src="js/controllers.js"></script>
<script src="js/services.js"></script>
```

```
</head>
<body>
<div ng-view></div>
</body>
</html>
```

Modifying App.js

The newly created services module must be added to the application before it can be used. We add the new `blogServices` module as a dependency of the application at startup time using inline array annotations, as shown here. Now the new services can be injected and used in controllers whenever needed. We can now replace the hardcoded JSON used as mock data in previous chapters:

```
/* chapter7/app.js */

'use strict';
/* App Module */

var blogApp = angular.module('blogApp', [
  'ngRoute',
  'blogControllers',
  'blogServices'
]);

blogApp.config(['$routeProvider', '$locationProvider',
  function($routeProvider, $locationProvider) {
    $routeProvider.
      when('/', {
      templateUrl: 'partials/main.html',
      controller: 'BlogCtrl'
    }).when('/blogPost/:id', {
      templateUrl: 'partials/blogPost.html',
      controller: 'BlogViewCtrl'
  });

  $locationProvider.html5Mode(false).hashPrefix('!');
}]);
```

Modifying the Controllers

Now let's see how to use the new services in our controllers. Replace the previous code in *controllers.js* with the code shown next. The code shows how we inject the services into each controller. We populate the scope properties inside the success callback function, as explained in previous chapters.

As explained earlier, the success callback function is only called when the REST service call returns successfully. At that point, we can safely populate the scope properties. The scope properties are then bound to the view by the AngularJS framework:

```
/* chapter7/controllers.js */

'use strict';
/* Controllers */

var blogControllers =
  angular.module('blogControllers', []);

blogControllers.controller('BlogCtrl',
  ['$scope', 'BlogList',
    function BlogCtrl($scope, BlogList) {
      BlogList.get({},
        function success(response) {
          console.log("Success:" + JSON.stringify(response));
          $scope.blogList = response;
      },
        function error(errorResponse) {
          console.log("Error:" + JSON.stringify(errorResponse));
      });
}]);

blogControllers.controller('BlogViewCtrl',
  ['$scope', '$routeParams', 'BlogPost',
    function BlogViewCtrl($scope, $routeParams, BlogPost) {
      var blogId = $routeParams.id;
      BlogPost.get({id: blogId},
        function success(response) {
        console.log("Success:" + JSON.stringify(response));
        $scope.blogEntry = response;
      },
        function error(errorResponse) {
          console.log("Error:" + JSON.stringify(errorResponse));
      });
}]);
```

We also made some changes to the *controllers.js* file to make testing easier. Testing AngularJS controllers can be more complex when REST services are involved. As mentioned previously, we don't know when REST services will return results, because they are asynchronous calls.

Asynchronous REST service calls will always cause controller unit tests to fail. Unit tests of controllers that depend on REST services will finish execution before the REST services ever return results, so any scope properties used by controller unit tests will be missing when the test script executes if those properties are returned from a REST service call.

There are ways to add a delay and make unit test scripts wait on the REST service results, but they add an unneeded level of complexity to the test scripts. Unit testing, after all, should be a test of a unit of code and not an end-to-end test. Protractor E2E tests are a better way to test REST services.

Look at the code that follows. The BlogList service is injected into the BlogCtrl controller. We make an asynchronous call to the get method of the BlogList service by passing two callback functions to the call. The success callback function returns a successful service response object, and the error callback function returns any errors if the service call fails:

```
/* chapter7/controllers.js excerpt */

blogControllers.controller('BlogCtrl', ['$scope', 'BlogList',
    function BlogCtrl($scope, BlogList) {
      $scope.blogList = [];
        BlogList.get({},
          function success(response) {
            console.log("Success:" + JSON.stringify(response));
            $scope.blogList = response;
          },
          function error(errorResponse) {
            console.log("Error:" + JSON.stringify(errorResponse));
          }
        );
}]);
```

It may take a second or more for the REST service to return results. Once the REST service does return results, the success callback function will be called. Unfortunately, the unit test script will have finished execution long before. We remedy this issue by making a change to the controller.

Notice the assignment $scope.blogList = []; in the preceding code. The assignment has no impact on the functionality of the controller, but it has a major impact on the unit test script associated with the BlogCtrl controller. The assignment initializes the scope blogList property with an empty array.

The following code shows how the empty array is used to test the blogCtrl controller. Notice the line of code checks that the array length is equal to 0:

```
/* chapter7/controllerSpec.js excerpt */

expect(scope.blogList.length).toEqual(0);
```

We can then rest assured that the controller is working successfully from a "unit of code" perspective. You will see later how to make sure the REST service worked as expected.

Running the Application

In NetBeans, right-click and run your AngularJS blog application. You should see the same data displayed on the screen that was there when the data was hardcoded. If you are using Chrome as your browser, you can turn on "Developer Tools" and click the "Network" menu button to see the REST service calls that are made as you click various links in the application. You can also click the Headers, Preview, Response, and Timing tabs in Developer Tools to see specific information about each service call.

Using Chrome Developer Tools is also a great way to troubleshoot issues with AngularJS REST service calls if you have problems. There's a great JavaScript debugger that can be used to debug REST service calls and other JavaScript issues.

If you are not familiar with Chrome Developer Tools, see the Google Chrome site (*https://developer.chrome.com/devtools*) for more information. In addition to the Chrome debugger, NetBeans also has a debugger built in for debugging JavaScript applications. For more information on debugging JavaScript in NetBeans, take a look at the NetBeans website.

Testing Services with Karma

The best way to test AngularJS services is with Karma. We used Karma as one of our test frameworks in previous chapters. You should have already created the *package.json* file for the blog project back in Chapter 5. The file is shown again here for reference:

```
/* chapter7/package.json */

{
    "name": "package.json",
    "devDependencies": {
        "karma": "*",
        "karma-chrome-launcher": "*",
        "karma-firefox-launcher": "*",
        "karma-jasmine": "*",
        "karma-junit-reporter": "*",
        "karma-coverage": "*"
    }
}
```

We also created the Karma configuration file for the blog project back in Chapter 5, but we need to make a small change to that: we need to add the AngularJS *angular-resource.min.js* file to the *karma.conf.js* file to test our services. The *angular-resource.min.js* file is used by both the BlogList and BlogPost services. The modified *karma.conf.js* file looks like this:

```
/* chapter7/karma.conf.js */
```

```
module.exports = function (config) {
    config.set({
        basePath: '../',
        files: [
            "public_html/js/libs/angular.min.js",
            "public_html/js/libs/angular-mocks.js",
            "public_html/js/libs/angular-route.min.js",
            "public_html/js/libs/angular-resource.min.js",
            "public_html/js/*.js",
            "test/**/*Spec.js"
        ],
        exclude: [
        ],
        autoWatch: true,
        frameworks: [
            "jasmine"
        ],
        browsers: [
            "Chrome",
            "Firefox"
        ],
        plugins: [
            "karma-junit-reporter",
            "karma-chrome-launcher",
            "karma-firefox-launcher",
            "karma-jasmine"
        ]
    });
};
```

Karma Service Specifications

Now we need to add new service test specifications for the blog project. Do the following:

1. Create a new JavaScript file named *servicesSpec.js* under the *unit* folder.

2. Enter the following code in the new file:

```
/* chapter7/servicesSpec.js */

/* Jasmine specs for controllers */
describe('AngularJS Blog Service Testing', function () {
  describe('test BlogList', function () {
    var $rootScope;
    var blogList;

    beforeEach(module('blogServices'));
    beforeEach(inject(function ($injector) {
      $rootScope = $injector.get('$rootScope');
      blogList = $injector.get('BlogList');
    }));
```

```
    it('should test BlogList service', function () {
      expect(blogList).toBeDefined();
    });
  });
  describe('test BlogPost', function () {
    var $rootScope;
    var blogPost;
    beforeEach(module('blogServices'));
    beforeEach(inject(function ($injector) {
      $rootScope = $injector.get('$rootScope');
      blogPost = $injector.get('BlogPost');
    }));
    it('should test BlogPost service', function () {
      expect(blogPost).toBeDefined();
    });
  });
});
```

It is important to point out here that our test specifications for the blog services do not depend on the presence and functionality of the associated REST services that get called by those services. Karma unit tests should test that the AngularJS services can be injected. If the tests are successful, that proves that the services are constructed properly. Our unit testing of services does not, however, prove that the REST services are working.

As I mentioned before, Karma unit tests often run inside some continuous integration (CI) framework. CI systems are often configured to trigger the running of unit tests every time a change is pushed to the source repository. The existence and accessibility of REST services can't always be guaranteed when you're unit testing inside a CI.

Unit tests shouldn't depend on the existence of REST services or other network-related devices. Unit testing should test the individual units of code and not try to do end-to-end testing. We will test the functionality of our REST services when we do E2E testing with Protractor. Any problems related to the calling of REST services will show as failures in Protractor.

Karma Testing

The new test specifications will unit test the new services. The controllers will also be tested because we still have the *controllerSpec.js* file in our system. Our Karma configuration file looks for all test files that end in *Spec.js*.

Right-click the project and select "Test" from the menu. Karma will start. You should see both Chrome and Firefox browser windows open. The NetBeans test results window should open and display four passed tests for Chrome and four passed tests for Firefox.

If you get any error messages or failed tests, go back over this section and verify that you completed all the configurations and installations. You can also download the Chapter 7 code from the GitHub project site (*https://github.com/KenWilliamson*).

End-to-End Testing

We already created a Protractor configuration file for the blog application in Chapter 5. The Protractor configuration file is shown here for reference:

```
/* chapter7/conf.js Protractor configuration file */

exports.config = {
  seleniumAddress: 'http://localhost:4444/wd/hub',
  specs: ['e2e/blog-spec.js']
};
```

Protractor Test Specification

Now we need to change the Protractor test specifications created earlier. The new Protractor tests need to interact with the REST services that we use in this chapter.

Copy the code shown here into the *blog-spec.js* file. Make sure the lines like browser.get("http://localhost:8383/AngularJsBlog/"); match the URL that you use on your system to call the blog application. The URL can be different for different development environments and can depend on how you named your project:

```
/* chapter7/blog-spec.js Protractor test specification */

describe("Blog Application Test", function(){
    it("should test the main blog page", function(){

        browser.get(
        "http://localhost:8383/AngularJsBlogChapter7/");
        expect(browser.getTitle()).toEqual("AngularJS Blog");

        //gets the blog list
        var blogList =
         element.all(by.repeater('blogPost in blogList'));

        //tests the size of the blogList
        expect(blogList.count()).toEqual(1);
        browser.get(
         "http://localhost:8383/AngularJsBlogChapter7
           /#!/blogPost/5394e59c4f50850000e6b7ea");
        expect(browser.getTitle()).toEqual("AngularJS Blog");

        //gets the comment list
        var commentList =
        element.all(by.repeater('comment in blogEntry.comments'));
```

```
        //checks the size of the commentList
        expect(commentList.count()).toEqual(2);
    });
});
```

Protractor Testing

Start a new command window and enter the following command to start the test server:

```
webdriver-manager start
```

Open a new command window and navigate to the root of the Chapter 5 project. Type the command:

```
protractor test/conf.js
```

You should see a browser window open. You should then see the test script navigate through the pages of the blog application. When the Protractor script has finished, the browser window will close.

You should see results like the following in the command window when the Protractor script completes. The number of seconds that it takes the script to finish will vary depending on your particular system:

```
Finished in 1.52 seconds
1 test, 4 assertions, 0 failures
```

Conclusion

This concludes our discussion of AngularJS models. We added code to make our blog application work with REST services running in the cloud, and we wrote unit tests to test the new services that we added. We then used Protractor to do end-to-end testing that validated the functionality of our REST services and the AngularJS services associated with those REST services.

We will talk about models again in Chapter 11, when we deploy our application to the cloud as a MEAN stack application. Next, we will add some non-REST services to handle business logic and see the power of AngularJS in action.

Services and Business Logic

Not all AngularJS services connect to REST services. Services can also contain business logic that is used by multiple controllers. As I mentioned before, if the business logic can be moved to a REST service, that is where it should be defined. Defining business logic in REST services assures that the same logic will be readily available to all client-side applications.

Often, however, it is not possible to move all business logic to REST services. Often that same business logic is needed across multiple controllers. That is where AngularJS non-REST services come in handy once again. In this chapter we will look at several examples of where AngularJS non-REST services are useful.

Take, for example, a situation where a user needs to authenticate across multiple REST services. One way to do that is by using Basic Authentication, where the user's username and password are passed to a service as a token in the HTTPS header during a service call. The token is in the form of "username:password" and encoded with base64.

As we know, a REST service shouldn't hold state, and holding a user's credentials in a session variable on the server is a serious security concern. Using a session variable to hold authentication state on the server side is usually not acceptable in most REST service designs. AngularJS services are great for handling such situations.

Handling User Authentication

First, we need a way to validate a user's credentials over HTTPS. The following code shows a REST service used to authenticate a user:

```
/* chapter8/ login REST service URL from services.js */

POST: https://www.micbutton.com/user/login
```

Here is the JSON request for the REST service:

```
{
    "username":"ken",
    "password":"password"
}
```

And here is the JSON response for the REST service:

```
{
    "authenticated":true
}
```

This particular service call would normally be open to any user and therefore would not require authentication. Allowing all users to access this service uninhibited means any user can try to validate against the service. If there is a possibility of abuse, the service could be secured at the network level, or a challenge and response system could be used to discourage unwanted users.

Once a user makes a call to the login service and the user's credentials are validated, it is the job of the AngularJS application to temporarily store those credentials. It is also the job of the AngularJS application to direct the user to a login page when the user has not authenticated. AngularJS non-REST services play a major role in this process.

Using Basic Authentication

If the REST services are designed properly to require authentication on all services that contain private data, the AngularJS application user will never have access to private data without providing the proper credentials. Once the user provides valid user credentials, the AngularJS application can store those credentials in a cookie or some other temporary storage. Cookies are a good place to store user credentials because all modern browsers store cookies mapped to a particular web domain. Cookie access is then granted only to the application that actually created the cookie on that particular domain. Other JavaScript applications running in the browser only have access to cookies they create, which are associated with their respective domains.

Creating AngularJS Services

As I mentioned in Chapter 6, there are three ways to create services in AngularJS. A service can be created with the service function, as shown here:

```
/* chapter8/ service function */

var blogServices = angular.module('blogServices',
['ngResource']); blogServices.service('BlogPost', [...]
```

or with the provider function:

```
/* chapter8/ provider function */

var blogServices = angular.module('blogServices',
['ngResource']); blogServices.provider('BlogPost', […]
```

The third way to create services in AngularJS is with the factory function. This is the method we will use to create AngularJS services in this chapter and throughout this book, because it is the most commonly used method. The following code shows how to create a service with the factory function:

```
/* chapter8/ factory function */

var blogServices = angular.module('blogServices',
['ngResource']); blogServices.factory('BlogPost', […]
```

Holding User Credentials

Now let's take a look at an AngularJS business logic service designed to save the user's credentials once the user has authenticated. The service makes use of AngularJS cookies, which we can include in an application by including the *angular-cookies.min.js* library file. The service has two parameters defined: the username (un) and password (pw).

The two values assigned to the service are used to build the token that is sent in the HTTPS header of each REST service call. The AngularJS service then stores the token and the username as cookies for use later:

```
/* chapter8/ non-REST business service to set user credentials */

blogBusinessServices.factory('setCreds',
['$cookies', function($cookies) {
return function(un, pw) {
  var token = un.concat(":", pw);
    $cookies.blogCreds = token;
    $cookies.blogUsername = un;
  };
}]);
```

Here's what a call to the setCreds business logic service to save an authenticated user's credentials looks like:

```
/* chapter8/controllers.js excerpt */

setCreds($scope.username, $scope.password);
```

Checking User Credentials

Now let's look at a business logic service that checks the status of a user's credentials. If the service returns false, the AngularJS application should redirect the user to the login page. It is also important to remember to save the user's credentials by making a call to setCreds any time the user's password is changed:

```
/* chapter8/ non-REST business logic service to check credentials */

blogBusinessServices.factory('checkCreds',
['$cookies', function($cookies) {

  return function() {
    var returnVal = false;
    var blogCreds = $cookies.blogCreds;
    if (blogCreds !== undefined && blogCreds !== "") {
      returnVal = true;
    }

    return returnVal;
  };
}]);
```

The service simply looks for the existence of the blogCreds cookie and returns true if the cookie exists. If a subsequent service call fails with the saved credentials and returns an HTTP 401 error code, it is the job of the AngularJS application to delete the saved cookies and redirect the user to the login page. The following code shows a call to the checkCreds service:

```
/* chapter8/controllers.js excerpt */

if (checkCreds()){
// do something to continue
}
```

Deleting User Credentials

Our next service deletes the user's credentials once the user's session has ended, or when the user's credentials failed to authenticate during a REST service call. Once the blogCreds cookie is removed, the AngularJS application should redirect the user to the login page:

```
/* chapter8/ non-REST business logic service to delete credentials */

blogBusinessServices.factory('deleteCreds',
  ['$cookies', function($cookies) {
    return function() {
      $cookies.blogCreds = "";
      $cookies.blogUsername = "";
    };
}]);
```

Here's what a call to the deleteCreds service looks like:

```
/* chapter8/controllers.js excerpt */

deleteCreds();
```

Retrieving User Credentials

The following code shows a business logic service that retrieves the user's token from
the blogCreds cookie. A token passed to a REST service in the HTTPS header must
be encoded with base64. The business service encodes the token in base64 and then
returns that encoded token:

```
/* chapter8/ non-REST business logic service to retrieve credentials */

blogBusinessServices.factory('getToken',
  ['$cookies', function($cookies) {
    return function() {
      var returnVal = "";
      var blogCreds = $cookies.blogCreds;
      if (blogCreds !== undefined && blogCreds !== "") {
        returnVal = btoa(blogCreds);
      }
      return returnVal;
    };
}]);
```

The following code shows how the token returned from the service is used to build
the Basic Authentication header when we're calling a REST service. This line should
be defined before every REST service call that requires authentication. The call makes
use of the AngularJS $http service:

```
/* chapter8/controllers.js excerpt */

$http.defaults.headers.common['Authorization'] = 'Basic ' + getToken();
```

The following code shows how to use the getToken service to authenticate to the Blog
service when we are saving a blog post:

```
/* chapter8/controllers.js excerpt */

blogControllers.controller('NewBlogCtrl',
  ['$scope', 'checkCreds', '$location', '$http', 'getToken',
    function NewBlogCtrl($scope, checkCreds, $location, $http, getToken) {

      $http.defaults.headers.common['Authorization'] = 'Basic ' + getToken();

        Blog.save({},
      function success(response) {
        console.log("Success:" + JSON.stringify(response));
        $scope.status = response;
      },
      function error(errorResponse) {
```

```
      console.log("Error:" + JSON.stringify(errorResponse));
    }
  );
}]);
```

One final business logic service that would be useful is shown next. The service retrieves the user's username from the `blogUsername` cookie. The username is then returned for use in multiple places throughout the application. Using the `getUser name` service simplifies storing and accessing the user's username:

```
/* chapter8/ non-REST business logic service to retrieve username */

blogBusinessServices.factory('getUsername',
  ['$cookies', function($cookies) {
    return function() {
      var returnVal = "";
      var blogUsername = $cookies.blogUsername;
      if (blogUsername !== undefined && blogUsername !== "") {
        returnVal = blogUsername;
      }
      return returnVal;
    };
}]);
```

It should be obvious by now that AngularJS services are very valuable to have in an application. Any time AngularJS business logic needs to be used by multiple controllers, that logic should be defined in services.

We will now add everything that we have covered in this chapter into one file, called *businessServices.js*, and add the services in that file to our blog project. In Chapter 10 we will add a login screen and security to our blog application. With security in place, we will then deploy our application to the cloud in Chapter 11. Before we deploy our blog application to the cloud, however, we will add new screens in Chapter 11 to allow a user to submit new blog posts and comments.

Blog Application Business Logic

Now, to add the new business services, right-click the project node and add a new JavaScript file named *businessServices.js* under the *js* folder. Here is the code that should be placed in the newly created services file. Notice that we have made AngularJS cookies available by injecting `ngCookies`. AngularJS cookies are provided by *angular-cookies.min.js*, which we already added to the project earlier:

```
/* chapter8/businessServices.js */

'use strict';
/* business logic services only */

var blogBusinessServices =
```

```
angular.module('blogBusinessServices', ['ngCookies']);

blogBusinessServices.factory('checkCreds',
  ['$cookies', function($cookies) {
    return function() {
      var returnVal = false;
      var blogCreds = $cookies.blogCreds;
      if (blogCreds !== undefined && blogCreds !== "") {
        returnVal = true;
      }
      return returnVal;
    };
}]);

blogBusinessServices.factory('getToken',
  ['$cookies', function($cookies) {
    return function() {
      var returnVal = "";
      var blogCreds = $cookies.blogCreds;
      if (blogCreds !== undefined && blogCreds !== "") {
        returnVal = btoa(blogCreds);
      }
      return returnVal;
    };
}]);

blogBusinessServices.factory('getUsername',
  ['$cookies', function($cookies) {
    return function() {
      var returnVal = "";
      var blogUsername = $cookies.blogUsername;
      if (blogUsername !== undefined && blogUsername !== "") {
        returnVal = blogUsername;
      }
      return returnVal;
    };
}]);

blogBusinessServices.factory('setCreds',
  ['$cookies', function($cookies) {
    return function(un, pw) {
      var token = un.concat(":", pw);
      $cookies.blogCreds = token;
      $cookies.blogUsername = un;
    };
}]);

blogBusinessServices.factory('deleteCreds',
  ['$cookies', function($cookies) {
    return function() {
      $cookies.blogCreds = "";
      $cookies.blogUsername = "";
```

```
    };
}]);
```

Using the Business Logic

Now to load the new business logic services, we must add the *businessServices.js* file to the <head> section of *index.html*, as shown here:

```
<!-- chapter8/index.html excerpt -->

<script src="js/businessServices.js"></script>
```

The complete *index.html* file is shown here for convenience:

```
<!-- chapter8/index.html -->

<!DOCTYPE html>
<html lang="en" ng-app="blogApp">
<head>
<title>AngularJS Blog</title>
<meta name="viewport" content="width=device-width, initial-scale=1.0">
<meta http-equiv="Content-Type" content="text/html; charset=UTF-8">

<link rel="stylesheet" href="lib-css/bootstrap.min.css" media="screen"/>
<link rel="stylesheet" href="css/styles.css" media="screen"/>

<script src="js/libs/jquery-1.10.2.min.js"></script>
<script src="js/libs/bootstrap.min.js"></script>
<script src="js/libs/angular.min.js"></script>
<script src="js/libs/angular-route.min.js"></script>
<script src="js/libs/angular-resource.min.js"></script>
<script src="js/libs/angular-cookies.min.js"></script>
<script src="js/app.js"></script>
<script src="js/controllers.js"></script>
<script src="js/services.js"></script>
<script src="js/businessServices.js"></script>

</head>
<body>
<div ng-view></div>
</body>
</html>
```

We must also add the new blogBusinessServices module as a dependency of the application at startup time. We do this using inline array annotations:

```
/* chapter8/app.js */

'use strict';
/* App Module */

var blogApp = angular.module('blogApp', [
```

```
  'ngRoute',
  'blogControllers',
  'blogServices',
  'blogBusinessServices'
]);

blogApp.config(['$routeProvider', '$locationProvider',
  function($routeProvider, $locationProvider) {
    $routeProvider.
      when('/', {
        templateUrl: 'partials/main.html',
        controller: 'BlogCtrl'
      }).when('/blogPost/:id', {
        templateUrl: 'partials/blogPost.html',
        controller: 'BlogViewCtrl'
    });

    $locationProvider.html5Mode(false).hashPrefix('!');
}]);
```

Testing Services with Karma

Unit testing services is how we find defects early in the development process. In fact, unit tests for each individual service should be written when the service is written. Although our services in this chapter are not overly complicated, unit testing is still very important. We will continue to use Karma for unit testing in this chapter.

Karma Configuration

We already have a Karma configuration file for our blog project, but we need to make a modification to the file to accommodate AngularJS cookies in our Karma unit test scripts. Since the services in this chapter rely on AngularJS cookies, we need to make the *karma.conf.js* file aware of the *angular-cookies.min.js* file in our project.

The line in the *karma.conf.js* file that makes Karma aware of AngularJS cookies is shown here:

```
/* chapter8/karma.conf.js excerpt */

files: [
    ...
    "public_html/js/libs/angular-cookies.min.js",
    ...
],
```

The complete *karma.conf.js* file is shown here. Make the needed change to the *karma.conf.js* file in your blog project, and then we will look at how we test our new business services:

```
/* chapter8/karma.conf.js complete file */

module.exports = function (config) {
    config.set({
        basePath: '../',
        files: [
            "public_html/js/libs/angular.min.js",
            "public_html/js/libs/angular-mocks.js",
            "public_html/js/libs/angular-route.min.js",
            "public_html/js/libs/angular-resource.min.js",
            "public_html/js/libs/angular-cookies.min.js",
            "public_html/js/*.js",
            "test/**/*Spec.js"
        ],
        exclude: [
        ],
        autoWatch: true,
        frameworks: [
            "jasmine"
        ],
        browsers: [
            "Chrome",
            "Firefox"
        ],
        plugins: [
            "karma-junit-reporter",
            "karma-chrome-launcher",
            "karma-firefox-launcher",
            "karma-jasmine"
        ]
    });
};
```

Karma Test Specifications

Now we need to add unit test specifications for each of the five business logic services that we added earlier in the chapter. We will talk briefly about each individual unit test to gain a full understanding of the test specifications.

First we will take a look at the unit test for the setCreds service. If you remember, the setCreds service takes two parameters, the username and password. We will test the operation of the service thoroughly in the unit tests that follow, but for now our unit test will only check that the setCreds service can be injected:

```
/* chapter8/businessServicesSpec.js excerpt - setCreds service */

describe('test setCreds', function () {
  var $rootScope;
  var setCreds;

  beforeEach(module('blogBusinessServices'));
```

```
  beforeEach(inject(function ($injector) {
    $rootScope = $injector.get('$rootScope');
    setCreds = $injector.get('setCreds');
    setCreds("test", "test");
  }));

  it('should test setCreds service exist', function () {
    expect(setCreds).toBeDefined();
  });
});
```

Next we will look at the unit test for the checkCreds service. The unit test script uses both the setCreds service and the checkCreds service. Recall that the checkCreds service uses AngularJS cookies. When cookies are created from a unit test script, the cookies created exist only for the duration of the test script. When the unit test script ends, so do the cookies. Our checkCreds unit test looks like this:

```
/* chapter8/businessServicesSpec.js excerpt - checkCreds service */

describe('test checkCreds', function () {
    var $rootScope;
    var checkCreds;
    var setCreds;

    beforeEach(module('blogBusinessServices'));
    beforeEach(inject(function ($injector) {
      $rootScope = $injector.get('$rootScope');
      checkCreds = $injector.get('checkCreds');
      setCreds = $injector.get('setCreds');
      setCreds("test", "test");
    }));
    it('should test setCreds service exist', function () {
      expect(checkCreds()).toEqual(true);
    });
});
```

The test script first makes a call to the setCreds service, passing a username of "test" and a password of "test" as parameters. Those values are stored in a cookie valid only for this test script run. We then validate that the checkCreds service returns true, indicating that both the setCreds and checkCreds service calls were successful. We can now rest assured that both services are working as expected.

Now we will take a look at the unit test for the getToken service. Just as before, we make a call to the setCreds service and pass a username of "test" and a password of "test" to the service. We then make a call to the getToken service. The returned value from the service is a base64-encoded string that is composed of the username and the password. We will only validate that a value is returned, with the toBeDefined method:

```
/* chapter8/businessServicesSpec.js excerpt - getToken service */

describe('test getToken', function () {
  var $rootScope;
  var getToken;
  var setCreds;

  beforeEach(module('blogBusinessServices'));
  beforeEach(inject(function ($injector) {
    $rootScope = $injector.get('$rootScope');
    getToken = $injector.get('getToken');
    setCreds = $injector.get('setCreds');
    setCreds("test", "test");
  }));
  it('should test setCreds service exist', function () {
    expect(getToken()).toBeDefined();
  });
});
```

When we test the getUsername service, we can actually validate the value set for the username. The following code shows the unit test for the getUsername service. Just as before, we make a call to the setCreds service and pass a username of "test" and a password of "test." We then make a call to the getUsername service and validate that it returns "test" as the username:

```
/* chapter8/businessServicesSpec.js excerpt - getUsername service */

describe('test getUsername', function () {
  var $rootScope;
  var getUsername;
  var setCreds;

  beforeEach(module('blogBusinessServices'));
  beforeEach(inject(function ($injector) {
    $rootScope = $injector.get('$rootScope');
    getUsername = $injector.get('getUsername');
    setCreds = $injector.get('setCreds');
    setCreds("test", "test");
  }));
  it('should test setCreds service exist', function () {
    expect(getUsername()).toEqual("test");
  });
});
```

The last unit test is shown next. It is a test of the deleteCreds service. In this test script we make a call to the setCreds service, then we call the deleteCreds service to remove the credentials that we just added. We then call the checkCreds service to validate that no credentials are stored by checking for a returned value of false:

```
/* chapter8/businessServicesSpec.js excerpt - deleteCreds service */
```

```
describe('test deleteCreds', function () {
  var $rootScope;
  var deleteCreds;
  var setCreds;
  var checkCreds;
  beforeEach(module('blogBusinessServices'));
  beforeEach(inject(function ($injector) {
    $rootScope = $injector.get('$rootScope');
    deleteCreds = $injector.get('deleteCreds');
    setCreds = $injector.get('setCreds');
    checkCreds = $injector.get('checkCreds');
    setCreds("test", "test");
    deleteCreds();
  }));
  it('should test setCreds service exist', function () {
    expect(checkCreds()).toEqual(false);
  });
});
```

Following is the complete *businessServicesSpec.js* file. Right-click the *unit* folder under the *test* folder, create a new JavaScript file named *businessServicesSpec.js*, and enter the code shown here:

```
/* chapter8/businessServicesSpec.js complete file */

describe('AngularJS Blog Business Service Testing', function () {
  describe('test setCreds', function () {
    var $rootScope;
    var setCreds;
    beforeEach(module('blogBusinessServices'));
    beforeEach(inject(function ($injector) {
      $rootScope = $injector.get('$rootScope');
      setCreds = $injector.get('setCreds');
      setCreds("test", "test");
    }));
    it('should test setCreds service exist', function () {
      expect(setCreds).toBeDefined();
    });
  });

  describe('test checkCreds', function () {
    var $rootScope;
    var checkCreds;
    var setCreds;
    beforeEach(module('blogBusinessServices'));
    beforeEach(inject(function ($injector) {
      $rootScope = $injector.get('$rootScope');
      checkCreds = $injector.get('checkCreds');
      setCreds = $injector.get('setCreds');
      setCreds("test", "test");
    }));
```

```
    it('should test setCreds service exist', function ()
      expect(checkCreds()).toEqual(true);
    });
});

describe('test getToken', function () {
  var $rootScope;
  var getToken;
  var setCreds;
  beforeEach(module('blogBusinessServices'));
  beforeEach(inject(function ($injector) {
    $rootScope = $injector.get('$rootScope');
    getToken = $injector.get('getToken');
    setCreds = $injector.get('setCreds');
    setCreds("test", "test");
  }));
  it('should test setCreds service exist', function ()
    expect(getToken()).toBeDefined();
  });
});

describe('test getUsername', function () {
  var $rootScope;
  var getUsername;
  var setCreds;
  beforeEach(module('blogBusinessServices'));
  beforeEach(inject(function ($injector) {
    $rootScope = $injector.get('$rootScope');
    getUsername = $injector.get('getUsername');
    setCreds = $injector.get('setCreds');
    setCreds("test", "test");
  }));
  it('should test setCreds service exist', function () {
    expect(getUsername()).toEqual("test");
  });
});

describe('test deleteCreds', function () {
  var $rootScope;
  var deleteCreds;
  var setCreds;
  var checkCreds;
  beforeEach(module('blogBusinessServices'));
  beforeEach(inject(function ($injector) {
    $rootScope = $injector.get('$rootScope');
    deleteCreds = $injector.get('deleteCreds');
    setCreds = $injector.get('setCreds');
    checkCreds = $injector.get('checkCreds');
    setCreds("test", "test");
    deleteCreds();
  }));
  it('should test setCreds service exist', function () {
```

```
      expect(checkCreds()).toEqual(false);
    });
  });
});
```

Karma Testing

The preceding test specifications will test all the new business logic services added in this chapter. The controller test specification and the REST service test specification unit tests will also run when Karma starts.

Right-click the project and select "Test" from the menu. Karma will start. You should see both Chrome and Firefox browser windows open. The NetBeans test results window should open and display nine passed tests for Chrome and nine passed tests for Firefox.

If you get any error messages or failed tests, go back over this section and verify that you completed all the configurations and installations. You can also download the Chapter 8 code from the GitHub project site (*https://github.com/KenWilliamson*).

End-to-End Testing

We haven't yet added the business logic services created in this chapter to our controllers, so we should see no change in the end-to-end testing. We will validate that no adverse issues were introduced in this chapter with Protractor.

Protractor Configuration

We already created a Protractor configuration file for the blog application in Chapter 5. The Protractor configuration file is shown here for reference:

```
/* chapter8/conf.js Protractor configuration file */

exports.config = {
 seleniumAddress: 'http://localhost:4444/wd/hub',
   specs: ['e2e/blog-spec.js']
};
```

Protractor Test Specification

No changes are required to the Protractor test specification, shown here for reference:

```
/* chapter8/blog-spec.js Protractor test specification */

describe("Blog Application Test", function(){
  it("should test the main blog page", function(){
    browser.get(
      "http://localhost:8383/AngularJsBlog/");
```

```
    expect(browser.getTitle()).toEqual("AngularJS Blog");
    //gets the blog list
    var blogList =
      element.all(by.repeater('blogPost in blogList'));
    //tests the size of the blogList
    expect(blogList.count()).toEqual(1);

    browser.get(
      "http://localhost:8383/AngularJsBlog/
       #!/blogPost/5394e59c4f50850000e6b7ea");
      expect(browser.getTitle()).toEqual("AngularJS Blog");
      //gets the comment list
      var commentList =
        element.all(by.repeater('comment in blogEntry.comments'));
      //checks the size of the commentList
      expect(commentList.count()).toEqual(2);
    });
  });
```

Protractor Testing

Start a new command window and enter this command to start the test server:

```
webdriver-manager start
```

Open a new command window and navigate to the root of the Chapter 5 project. Type the command:

```
protractor test/conf.js
```

You should see a browser window open. You should then see the test script navigate through the pages of the blog application. When the Protractor script has finished, the browser window will close.

You should see results like the following in the command window when the Protractor script completes. The number of seconds that it takes the script to finish will vary depending on your particular system:

```
Finished in 1.768 seconds
1 test, 4 assertions, 0 failures
```

Conclusion

The changes to our blog application made in this chapter give us everything we need to enable us to work with REST service authentication. As mentioned before, our AngularJS application doesn't actually handle authentication, but instead holds the status of authentication.

The business logic services that we added in this chapter greatly simplify the process of tracking authentication across multiple controllers. We will talk more about security in Chapter 10. We will now move on to AngularJS directives.

AngularJS Directives

From a user's perspective, directives are nothing more than custom HTML tags that are added to application templates. Directives can be simple, or they can be very complex. Directives are used by the AngularJS HTML compiler to enhance the functionality of the associated template. Some examples of AngularJS directives are `ngModel`, `ngView`, and `ngRepeat`.

The HTML Compiler

Let's talk briefly about the AngularJS HTML compiler. The use of the word *compiler* in relation to AngularJS is often confusing for experienced developers new to the framework. Experienced developers don't normally associate compilers with HTML. The word *compiler*, however, takes on a whole new meaning in the context of AngularJS.

Compiling HTML in AngularJS is simply the process of searching through the DOM tree to identify HTML elements associated with directives. The compiler then builds the template and assigns events to the associated elements in the template. This, however, is a greatly simplified description of the AngularJS HTML compiler and the compiler processes. If you would like to know more about the compiler, take a look at the AngularJS website documentation, which covers the HTML compiler in great detail.

What Are Directives?

Directives are very valuable in AngularJS and are what sets AngularJS apart from most JavaScript client-side frameworks. Thanks to directives, we can avoid creating model classes with hundreds of lines of code. Thanks to directives, we have a simplified model and view in AngularJS that allows developers to quickly create powerful JavaScript applications.

Although building custom directives in AngularJS is a bit more complex to learn than other areas of the framework, I will try to simplify the learning process by showing you how to create a fairly simple directive. There are complete books that cover the AngularJS directive design process, so if you have a desire to learn about AngularJS directives in great detail, a book that covers only directives would be a good starting point after you finish this chapter.

Building Custom Directives

If you remember back in Chapter 5, we built a menu for our blog application and used `<div ng-include src="'partials/menu.html'"></div>` to include that menu into each template. The menu was defined in the *menu.html* file as HTML. While that approach works well and is a common way to add an application menu, there is another way to add a menu that is a bit more elegant.

Our new menu approach will involve building a custom directive to handle the inclusion of a menu into our templates. First we must add a new directives file to our blog project. We then define the new directive and inject the directive into our application. Once that is done, we can replace `<div ng-include src="'partials/ menu.html'"></div>` with a tag that uses our custom directive.

Open your editor, right-click the application node, and create a new JavaScript file named *directives.js* under the *js* folder. The code to place in the file is shown next. We will walk through the code, and I'll explain how the directive actually works. We will then configure our blog application to use the new directive and see it in action:

```
/* chapter9/directives.js */

'use strict';
/* Directives */

var blogDirectives =
  angular.module('blogDirectives', []);

  blogDirectives.directive('blgMenu', function () {
    return {
      restrict: 'A',
      templateUrl: 'partials/menu.html',
      link: function (scope, el, attrs) {
      scope.label = attrs.menuTitle;
    }
  };
});
```

First we must create a new module named `blogDirectives`. We will then create a new directive on that module. We pass both the directive name and a callback function to the directives call on the `blogDirectives` module.

Naming Conventions for Directives

Take notice of the camel case directive name `blgMenu`. Since HTML is case-insensitive, we refer to the new directive inside an HTML template file as `blg-menu`. The AngularJS HTML compiler then normalizes the directive name into its camel case equivalent, `blgMenu`.

Also take notice of the `blg` prefix on the new directive name. All directive names used in templates must be unique. Directive names cannot match any existing HTML tag name, or any future HTML tag name. Custom directives also cannot use the `ng` prefix already used by AngularJS directives.

So, we must use a unique directive name that won't conflict with current or future HTML names or with AngularJS directive names. The best way to do that is to use a unique name prefix for custom directives. We will use `blg` for our prefix because it is unlikely to cause a problem now or in the future.

The Restrict Option

Also take notice of the line `restrict: 'A'` in our directive. That is known as the *restrict option*. The restrict option is how AngularJS triggers the directive inside a template. The value of "A" causes the directive to be triggered on the attribute name. The following table shows all the possible values for the restrict option. The default value for the restrict option is `'A'`.

Table 9-1. Restrict option

Value	Usage in AngularJS
`'A'`	Only match the attribute name (`<div blg-menu></div>`) (default)
`'E'`	Only match the element name (`<blg-menu></blg-menu>`)
`'C'`	Only match the class name (`<div class="blg-menu"></div>`)
`'M'`	Only match the comment name (`<!-- directive: blg-menu -->`)

The Template URL

Also notice the attribute assignment `templateUrl: 'partials/menu.html'`. The `templateUrl` attribute tells the AngularJS HTML compiler to replace the directive `blg-menu` inside a template with HTML content located inside a separate file. The `blg-menu` attribute will be replaced with the content of our original menu template file (*partials/menu.html*).

There is one small change that needs to be made in the menu template file to allow us to pass the site title to the directive as an argument. I will show that change shortly. Passing the title as an argument is not required or even needed, but I show it here to help explain how directives work.

Template Attributes

The following code shows how we pass `menu-title` as an argument to our new directive. All values are passed to the method named `link` as a parameter named `attrs`. We gain access to the title value by assigning the value of `attrs.menuTitle` to a scope property:

```
/* chapter9/directives.js excerpt */

link: function (scope, el, attrs) {
    scope.label = attrs.menuTitle;
}
```

The scope is passed as an argument to the `link` method and is accessible inside the method, as seen by the assignment of the `menuTitle` attribute. Directives are used inside a template as shown next, in the *main.html* template. `blg-menu` is the name of the directive, and `menu-title` is the name passed to the directive as the title attribute of the new directive. The AngularJS HTML compiler also normalizes the attribute name into its camel case form, so it becomes `menuTitle` inside the template (as shown before in the template code from *directives.js*):

```
<!-- chapter9/main.html excerpt -->

<div blg-menu menu-title="AngularJS Blog"></div>
```

Adding the Custom Directive

Now we must configure our blog application to use the newly created custom directive. To load the new directives file, we need to add one line in the *index.html* file:

```
<!-- chapter9/index.html excerpt -->

<script src="js/directives.js"></script>
```

The complete *index.html* file is shown here for convenience:

```html
<!-- chapter9/index.html -->

<!DOCTYPE html>
<html lang="en" ng-app="blogApp">
<head>
<title>AngularJS Blog</title>
<meta name="viewport" content="width=device-width, initial-scale=1.0">
<meta http-equiv="Content-Type" content="text/html; charset=UTF-8">

<link rel="stylesheet" href="lib-css/bootstrap.min.css" media="screen"/>
<link rel="stylesheet" href="css/styles.css" media="screen"/>

<script src="js/libs/jquery-1.10.2.min.js"></script>
<script src="js/libs/bootstrap.min.js"></script>
<script src="js/libs/angular.min.js"></script>
<script src="js/libs/angular-route.min.js"></script>
<script src="js/libs/angular-resource.min.js"></script>
<script src="js/libs/angular-cookies.min.js"></script>

<script src="js/app.js"></script>
<script src="js/controllers.js"></script>
<script src="js/services.js"></script>
<script src="js/businessServices.js"></script>
<script src="js/directives.js"></script>

</head>
<body>
<div ng-view></div>
</body>
</html>
```

We also need to make a change to the *app.js* file. We add the new `blogDirectives` module as a dependency of the application at startup time, using inline array annotations:

```js
/* chapter9/app.js */

'use strict';
/* App Module */

var blogApp = angular.module('blogApp', [
  'ngRoute',
  'blogControllers',
  'blogServices',
  'blogBusinessServices',
  'blogDirectives'
]);

blogApp.config(['$routeProvider', '$locationProvider',
  function($routeProvider, $locationProvider) {
    $routeProvider.
```

```
    when('/', {
      templateUrl: 'partials/main.html',
      controller: 'BlogCtrl'
    }).when('/blogPost/:id', {
      templateUrl: 'partials/blogPost.html',
      controller: 'BlogViewCtrl'
    });

  $locationProvider.html5Mode(false).hashPrefix('!');
}]);
```

Now we must modify our template files to use the newly created custom directive. In the *main.html* template file, we replace the line <div ng-include src="'partials/menu.html'"> </div> with the line shown here:

```
<!-- chapter9/main.html excerpt -->

<div blg-menu menu-title="AngularJS Blog"></div>
```

The complete *main.html* file is shown here for convenience:

```
<!-- chapter9/main.html -->

<div blg-menu menu-title="AngularJS Blog"></div>

<div id="container" class="container">

<div class="blog-post-label">Blog Posts</div>
<div class="post-wrapper">
<div ng-repeat="blogPost in blogList">

<div class="blog-post-outer">
<div class="blog-intro-text">
Posted: {{blogPost.date | date:'MM/dd/yyyy @ h:mma'}}
</div>
<div class="blog-intro-text">
{{blogPost.introText}}
</div>

<div class="blog-read-more">
<a href="#!blogPost/{{blogPost._id}}">Read More</a>
</div>
</div>
</div>

</div>
</div>
```

We make the same change to the *blogPost.html* template, as shown here:

```
<!-- chapter9/blogPost.html -->

<div blg-menu menu-title="AngularJS Blog"></div>
```

```
<div id="container" class="container">
<div class="blog-post-label">Blog Entry</div>
<div class="blog-entry-wrapper">

<div class="blog-intro-text">
Posted: {{blogEntry.date| date:'MM/dd/yyyy @ h:mma'}}
</div>
<div class="blog-entry-outer">
{{blogEntry.blogText}}
</div>

<div class="blog-comment-wrapper">
<div class="blog-comment-label">Blog Comments</div>
<div class="blog-entry-comments" ng-repeat="comment in blogEntry.comments">
{{comment.commentText}}
</div>

</div>
</div>
</div>
```

Passing the Title Attribute

Finally, we must make one last change to the *menu.html* template file to make use of the title value passed to the directive in the menu-title attribute. Replace the hardcoded title with {{label}}, as shown here:

```
<!-- chapter9/menu.html -->

<nav class="navbar navbar-inverse navbar-fixed-top" role="navigation">
<!-- Brand and toggle get grouped for better mobile display -->
<div class="container">
<div class="navbar-header">
<button type="button"
class="navbar-toggle" data-
toggle="collapse"
  data-target=".navbar-collapse">
<span class="sr-only">Toggle navigation</span>
<span class="icon-bar"></span>
<span class="icon-bar"></span>
<span class="icon-bar"></span>
</button>

<a class="navbar-brand" style="{{brandColor}}" href="#!/">{{label}}</a>
</div>

<!--Collect the nav links, forms, and other content for toggling -->
<div class="collapse navbar-collapse">
<ul class="nav navbar-nav">
<li class="{{aboutActiveClass}}"><a href="#!about">About</a></li>
```

```
<li class="">
<a href="https://github.com/KenWilliamson">Download Project Code</a>
</li>
</ul>

</div><!-- /.navbar-collapse -->
</div>
</nav>
```

With this change made, we can run the application and test our new menu.

Running the Blog Application

Now we will run our blog project to check that all changes were made successfully. Save all your changes and right-click the project node. Select "Run" from the menu, and the application should launch. If all changes were made correctly, you should see the menu bar across the top of the page just as before.

Turn on developer tools for your browser and check for any errors. If you have any problems, go over what we covered and validate that all the changes were made correctly. If you have issues that can't be resolved, download the code for Chapter 9 from the project site (*https://github.com/KenWilliamson*). Run the downloaded project to see the changes made in this chapter, and compare it to your code to find and fix any issues.

Testing Directives with Karma

Writing a test specification for a directive that uses an external HTML template file is a bit more complicated than writing most test specifications. The test script will fail when it tries to load the template file using HTTP from the server. If you were to use hardcoded HTML for the menu inside the directive, everything would work fine. Not so with external HTML templates, however.

One way around the problem is to use a preprocessor that converts our HTML template file into a JavaScript string and then generates an AngularJS module from that string. The preprocessed module is then loaded into the $templateCache and made available to Karma. That way we can use the cached version of our template file and our directive works as expected.

One way to handle the preprocessing is to use the karma-ng-html2js-preprocessor Karma plugin. Although the plugin is a bit tricky to configure properly, it quickly solves the external template problem. Pay particular attention to the way the plugin is configured. If you are using an IDE other than NetBeans, you may need to look for documentation specific to your IDE.

Karma Configuration

First, we need to edit the *package.json* file used to configure Node.js dependencies. Here is the needed change:

```
/* chapter9/package.json excerpt */

"karma-ng-html2js-preprocessor": "~0.1"
```

The complete *package.json* file is shown next. The added line makes the `karma-ng-html2js-preprocessor` plugin a Node.js dependency. The module is then accessible to Karma. Edit the existing blog project *package.json* file and add the required line as shown:

```
{
    "name": "package.json",
    "devDependencies": {
        "karma": "*",
        "karma-chrome-launcher": "*",
        "karma-firefox-launcher": "*",
        "karma-jasmine": "*",
        "karma-junit-reporter": "*",
        "karma-coverage": "*",
        "karma-ng-html2js-preprocessor": "~0.1"
    }
}
```

After we change the *package.json* file, we need to use npm to install the plugin.

Open a new command window and navigate to the root of the Chapter 9 project. You should see the *package.json* file when you list out the files in the folder.

Now type the following command to install the `karma-ng-html2js-preprocessor` plugin defined in the *package.json* file:

```
npm install
```

We need to make several changes to the *karma.conf.js* file that we created earlier. The changes are configuration changes for the new plugin just installed; they are subtle but important.

First, notice in the following code that we've added a new line in the `files` section. The new line, `'public_html/partials/*.html'`, tells the plugin where to find the template file used in our directive:

```
/* chapter9/karma.conf.js excerpt */

files: [
  "public_html/js/libs/angular.min.js",
  "public_html/js/libs/angular-mocks.js",
  "public_html/js/libs/angular-route.min.js",
  "public_html/js/libs/angular-resource.min.js",
```

```
    "public_html/js/libs/angular-cookies.min.js",
    "public_html/js/*.js",
    "public_html/partials/*.html",
    "test/**/*Spec.js"
]
```

We must also add a `preprocessors` section to the file. The entry in this section maps the location of the template files to the new Karma plugin:

```
/* chapter9/karma.conf.js excerpt */

preprocessors: {
  'public_html/partials/*.html': ['ng-html2js']
}
```

Next, we need to add the new plugin to the list of Karma plugins, as shown here—the last line tells Karma that this plugin will be used:

```
/* chapter9/karma.conf.js excerpt */

plugins: [
  "karma-junit-reporter",
  "karma-chrome-launcher",
  "karma-firefox-launcher",
  "karma-jasmine",
  "karma-ng-html2js-preprocessor"
]
```

There is one more change that we need to make to the *karma.conf.js* file. We need to tell the new plugin to strip `"public_html/"` from the path to the template files:

```
/* chapter9/karma.conf.js excerpt */

ngHtml2JsPreprocessor: {
  stripPrefix: 'public_html/'
}
```

Following is the complete modified *karma.conf.js* file. Open the *karma.conf.js* file in the blog project and make the needed changes:

```
/* chapter9/karma.conf.js complete file */

module.exports = function (config) {
  config.set({
    basePath: '../',
      files: [
        "public_html/js/libs/angular.min.js",
        "public_html/js/libs/angular-mocks.js",
        "public_html/js/libs/angular-route.min.js",
        "public_html/js/libs/angular-resource.min.js",
        "public_html/js/libs/angular-cookies.min.js",
        "public_html/js/*.js",
        "public_html/partials/*.html",
        "test/**/*Spec.js"
```

```
    ],
    preprocessors: {
      'public_html/partials/*.html': ['ng-html2js']
    },
    exclude: [
    ],
    autoWatch: true,
    frameworks: [
      "jasmine"
    ],
    browsers: [
      "Chrome",
      "Firefox"
    ],
    plugins: [
      "karma-junit-reporter",
      "karma-chrome-launcher",
      "karma-firefox-launcher",
      "karma-jasmine",
      "karma-ng-html2js-preprocessor"
    ],
    ngHtml2JsPreprocessor: {
      stripPrefix: 'public_html/'
    }
  });
};
```

Karma Test Specification

Now we need to add a new test specification to the blog project. Do the following:

1. Right-click the *unit* folder under the *test* folder and add a new JavaScript file named *directivesSpec.js* to the project.

2. Copy this code into the new *directivesSpec.js* file:

```
/* chapter9/directivesSpec.js */

describe('AngularJS Blog Application', function () {

    beforeEach(module('blogDirectives'));

    describe('Unit test of Menu Directive', function () {
        var rootScope, compile;

        // The external template file referenced by templateUrl
        beforeEach(module('partials/menu.html'));

        beforeEach(inject(function (_$compile_, _$rootScope_) {

            compile = _$compile_;
            rootScope = _$rootScope_;
```

```
        }));

    it('Replaces the menu attribute with the menu', function () {

        var elm = angular.element(
      "<div blg-menu menu-title=\"AngularJS Blog\"></div>");
        var menu = compile(elm)(rootScope);

        rootScope.$digest();

        expect(menu.html()).toContain("AngularJS Blog");

    });
  });

});
```

This code differs a bit from the test specifications that we have seen so far. Remember that directives need to be compiled by the HTML compiler. The test specification accounts for that need.

First, notice in the line shown here that we load the AngularJS module that represents the template HTML file that is needed by the directive. Remember that the template HTML file was converted to a JavaScript string, and then that string was used by the Karma preprocessor plugin to generate an AngularJS module:

```
/* chapter9/directivesSpec.js excerpt */

// The external template file referenced by templateUrl
beforeEach(module('partials/menu.html'));
```

Also notice that we now inject the HTML compiler with _$compile_. We also inject the rootScope with _$rootScope_:

```
/* chapter9/directivesSpec.js excerpt */

beforeEach(inject(function (_$compile_, _$rootScope_) {

    compile = _$compile_;
    rootScope = _$rootScope_;

}));
```

Recall that when we included our new directive inside the *main.html* template, we used the line <div blg-menu menu-title="AngularJS Blog"\></div> to include the new directive-based menu into the page. The following code shows that same line getting passed to the angular.element method:

```
/* chapter9/directivesSpec.js excerpt */

var elm = angular.
element("<div blg-menu menu-title=\"AngularJS Blog\"></div>");

var menu = compile(elm)(rootScope);
rootScope.$digest();
```

The resulting elm variable is then passed to the compiler along with the root scope reference, as shown here. Then we call $digest, and that tells AngularJS to update bindings and fire any watches.

Finally, we evaluate the HTML by calling the menu.html method and looking for the title that we passed to the directive with menu-title="AngularJS Blog".

Karma Testing

Now, with all the changes made to the blog project, we are ready to test our new directive.

Right-click the project and select "Test" from the menu. Karma will start. You should see both Chrome and Firefox browser windows open. The NetBeans test results window should open and display 10 passed tests for Chrome and 10 passed tests for Firefox.

If you get any error messages or failed tests, go back over this section and verify that you completed all the configurations and installations. You can also download the Chapter 9 code from the GitHub project site (*https://github.com/KenWilliamson*).

End-to-End Testing

We will make one small change to allow us to test the new directive-based menu during end-to-end testing. The modification will involve our Protractor test script clicking the main menu link after navigating to a blog entry.

Protractor Configuration

We already created a Protractor configuration file for the blog application in Chapter 5. The Protractor configuration file is shown here for reference:

```
/* chapter9/conf.js Protractor configuration file */

exports.config = {
  seleniumAddress: 'http://localhost:4444/wd/hub',
  specs: ['e2e/blog-spec.js']
};
```

Protractor Test Specification

We will make a small change to the test specification, shown next. Notice the last line in the file. The line uses the `navbar-brand` CSS class to look up the link to the main page. The script then clicks the link and navigates back to the main page. The test validates that the new menu is working correctly:

```
/* chapter9/blog-spec.js */

describe("Blog Application Test", function(){
  it("should test the main blog page", function(){
    browser.get("http://localhost:8383/AngularJsBlogChapter9/");
    expect(browser.getTitle()).toEqual("AngularJS Blog");

    //gets the blog list
    var blogList = element.all(by.repeater('blogPost in blogList'));

    //tests the size of the blogList
    expect(blogList.count()).toEqual(1);

    browser.get(
      "http://localhost:8383/AngularJsBlogChapter9/
      #!/blogPost/5394e59c4f50850000e6b7ea");
    expect(browser.getTitle()).toEqual("AngularJS Blog");

    //gets the comment list
    var commentList =
      element.all(by.repeater('comment in blogEntry.comments'));

    //checks the size of the commentList
    expect(commentList.count()).toEqual(2);
    element(by.css('.navbar-brand')).click();
  });
});
```

Protractor Testing

With those changes made, we are ready to start the end-to-end testing.

Start a new command window and enter this command to start the test server:

```
webdriver-manager start
```

Open a new command window and navigate to the root of the Chapter 9 project. Type the command:

```
protractor test/conf.js
```

You should see a browser window open. You should then see the test script navigate through the pages of the blog application. When the Protractor script has finished, the browser window will close.

You should see results like the following in the command window when the Protractor script completes. The number of seconds that it takes the script to finish will vary depending on your particular system:

```
Finished in 1.91 seconds
1 test, 4 assertions, 0 failures
```

Conclusion

In this chapter you learned how to create a custom AngularJS directive. You also learned how to write test specifications for AngularJS directives. We made all the needed changes to our blog application to add a new directive-based menu to our blog.

Once your blog application is running correctly, we can move on. This concludes our discussion of directives; we'll start adding security features to our blog application in the next chapter.

AngularJS Security

You might wonder why we are covering security in a book on AngularJS. Well, quite simply, security is one of the most important and most challenging tasks faced by an AngularJS developer. It's not that the developer is actually responsible for implementing the security layer—that is not the case at all—but it is very important for an AngularJS developer to understand the role that AngularJS plays in the overall security model of an application or website.

You should never attempt to implement an independent client-side security layer in an AngularJS application, or any other JavaScript application for that matter. Security should always be implemented on the backend services where the data resides. That is the only safe place to implement a security layer.

Remember the user has full access to the JavaScript running in the browser. As I said before, our AngularJS application runs in the user's browser on the user's hardware. The user can save the JavaScript locally and easily make modifications circumventing any security layer implemented by an unsuspecting JavaScript developer.

With that in mind, there are several rules that AngularJS developers and backend developers need to remember. Although actually implementing the security layer is not usually the job of an AngularJS developer, it is often a collaborative effort for all developers involved in a project. The following rules should always be considered:

1. Always use SSL to communicate with REST services that contain private data (HTTPS).

2. Always use some type of authentication on each REST service call that contains private data (Basic Authentication, for example).

3. Never hold REST service authentication status in a session variable on the server. Doing that opens your server-side application up to cross-origin attacks and other serious security concerns.

4. Never implement a Cross-Origin Resource Sharing (CORS) layer that returns * as the list of allowed domains. For example, (`Access-Control-Allow-Origin: *`) would allow all domains to make cross-origin calls to the REST services on the site. Doing that circumvents the browser's CORS security implementation completely.

5. Always make sure that any JavaScript that may get injected inside a JSON property does not get executed on the server side. This design flaw is at the core of the NoSQL injection attack, where JavaScript functions are injected in the JSON request of a service and unknowingly executed by the server, in order to breach the security of a NoSQL database.

Always remember that any security-related JavaScript code can be viewed and modified by the user. While most modern browsers do offer built-in security, JavaScript developers should never rely on the browser for security. The responsibility for security rests entirely on the shoulders of the backend service developers. With that said, I will show some techniques for developing AngularJS applications that work well with a security layer implemented properly in the backend services.

Authentication

We will start our discussion of security by building a login screen and the associated controller and service for our blog application. We will send the user's credentials to a login REST service for validation. We will also make use of the business logic services that we developed back in Chapter 8.

We don't actually use HTTPS for our blog application because it's not a production application. But in a production environment, SSL should always be used to protect private data and the user's credentials when calling a login REST service. Additional security steps could even be taken in the REST services to limit access to a particular machine or a particular IP address. We will not, however, be concerned with that level of security in this book.

Adding a Login Service

We will start off by adding an AngularJS login service. Open your editor and add the following code to the bottom of your project's *services.js* file. The new AngularJS login service maps to a login REST service on our backend server. The code is much like that of the other AngularJS services we've set up so far. It has one method, `login`, that maps to a `POST` method on the REST service:

```
/* chapter10/services.js excerpt */

blogServices.factory('Login', ['$resource',
  function($resource) {
    return
      $resource(
        "http://nodeblog-micbuttoncloud.rhcloud.com/NodeBlog/login",
          {}, {
      login: {method: 'POST', cache: false, isArray: false}
  });
}]);
```

Adding a Login Controller

Now we need to add a login controller. Open your editor and add the code shown
next to the bottom of the *controllers.js* file. Notice that we inject the new `Login` service
and the `setCreds` business logic service that we developed back in Chapter 8. We also
inject the `$location` service to allow us to redirect the user once authenticated. The
new controller has a `submit` method that is attached to the scope. Attaching the
method to the scope allows us to call the method from inside the login template. We
build the JSON request that gets passed to the service in the variable named `post`
`Data`, using the scope properties submitted by the form:

```
/* chapter10/controllers.js excerpt */

blogControllers.controller('LoginCtrl',
  ['$scope', '$location', 'Login', 'setCreds',
    function LoginCtrl($scope, $location, Login, setCreds) {
      $scope.submit = function(){
      $scope.sub = true;
      var postData = {
        "username" : $scope.username,
        "password" : $scope.password
      };

  Login.login({}, postData,
    function success(response) {
      console.log("Success:" + JSON.stringify(response));
      if(response.authenticated){
        setCreds($scope.username, $scope.password)
        $location.path('/');
      }else{
        $scope.error = "Login Failed"
      }
    },
    function error(errorResponse) {
      console.log("Error:" + JSON.stringify(errorResponse));
    }
  );
```

```
    };
  }]);
```

We also add a scope property named `error`. This property is populated any time the user fails to authenticate, displaying a "Login Failed" message. We will see how the error is presented later in the chapter. Once the user authenticates, we make a call to the AngularJS business logic service `setCreds` and pass the user's username and password to be saved in a cookie. We then redirect the user to the main application link.

Security Modifications to Other Controllers

We must also make minor modifications to the other two controllers in our blog project. Open your editor and replace the two controllers added earlier with the code shown next. Notice we now inject the `$location` service and the `checkCreds` business service that we added back in Chapter 8. The `checkCreds` service works by checking the user's credentials at the top of the controller. If the user has not authenticated, a call is made to the `path` method on the `$location` service to redirect the user to the login page (we will cover the new login path shortly):

```
/* chapter10/controllers.js excerpt */

blogControllers.controller('BlogCtrl',
  ['$scope', 'BlogList', '$location', 'checkCreds',
    function BlogCtrl($scope, BlogList, $location, checkCreds) {
      if(!checkCreds()){
        $location.path('/login');
      }

      BlogList.get({},
        function success(response) {
          console.log("Success:" + JSON.stringify(response));
          $scope.blogList = response;
        },
        function error(errorResponse) {
          console.log("Error:" + JSON.stringify(errorResponse));
        }
      );
  }]);


blogControllers.controller('BlogViewCtrl',
  ['$scope', '$routeParams', 'BlogPost', '$location', 'checkCreds',
    function BlogViewCtrl($scope, $routeParams, BlogPost,
      $location, checkCreds) {
      if(!checkCreds()){
        $location.path('/login');
      }
      var blogId = $routeParams.id;
```

```
BlogPost.get({id: blogId},
  function success(response) {
    console.log("Success:" + JSON.stringify(response));
    $scope.blogEntry = response;
  },
  function error(errorResponse) {
    console.log("Error:" + JSON.stringify(errorResponse));
  }
);
}]);
```

Adding a Logout Controller

We have one more change to make to the *controllers.js* file: we need to add a new con‐
troller to log the user out of the system and reset his credentials. Add the code shown
here to the bottom of the *controllers.js* file. Once again, we make use of the AngularJS
business logic services written back in Chapter 8 by adding a call to the deleteCreds
service. The service call removes the user's credentials, and then we redirect the user
to the login page:

```
/* chapter10/controllers.js excerpt */

blogControllers.controller('LogoutCtrl',
['$location', 'deleteCreds',
function LogoutCtrl($location, deleteCreds) {

  deleteCreds();
  $location.path('/login');

}]);
```

The entire *controllers.js* file is shown here to help make the changes clearer:

```
/* chapter10/controllers.js */

'use strict';
/* Controllers */

var blogControllers =
  angular.module('blogControllers', []);
blogControllers.controller('BlogCtrl',
  ['$scope', 'BlogList', '$location', 'checkCreds',
    function BlogCtrl($scope, BlogList, $location, checkCreds) {
      if(!checkCreds()){
        $location.path('/login');
      }

      BlogList.get({},
        function success(response) {
          console.log("Success:" + JSON.stringify(response));
```

```
            $scope.blogList = response;
          },
          function error(errorResponse) {
            console.log("Error:" + JSON.stringify(errorResponse));
          });
}]);

blogControllers.controller('BlogViewCtrl',
  ['$scope', '$routeParams', 'BlogPost', '$location', 'checkCreds',
    function BlogViewCtrl($scope, $routeParams, BlogPost,
      $location, checkCreds) {
        if(!checkCreds()){
          $location.path('/login');
        }
        var blogId = $routeParams.id;

        BlogPost.get({id: blogId},
          function success(response) {
            console.log("Success:" + JSON.stringify(response));
            $scope.blogEntry = response;
          },
          function error(errorResponse) {
            console.log("Error:" + JSON.stringify(errorResponse));
          });
}]);

blogControllers.controller('LoginCtrl',
  ['$scope', '$location','Login', 'setCreds',
    function LoginCtrl($scope, $location, Login, setCreds) {

      $scope.submit = function(){
      $scope.sub = true;
      var postData = {
        "username" : $scope.username,
        "password" : $scope.password
      };

      Login.login({}, postData,
        function success(response) {
          console.log("Success:" + JSON.stringify(response));
          if(response.authenticated){
            setCreds($scope.username, $scope.password)
            $location.path('/');
          }else{
            $scope.error = "Login Failed"
          }
        },
        function error(errorResponse) {
          console.log("Error:" + JSON.stringify(errorResponse));
        });
      };
}]);
```

```
blogControllers.controller('LogoutCtrl',
  ['$location', 'deleteCreds',
    function LogoutCtrl($location, deleteCreds) {
      deleteCreds();
      $location.path('/login');
}]);
```

Next, we will added a new login template and the associated CSS. We will then add two new paths to the $routeProvider section of the *app.js* file.

Adding a Login Template

Right-click the project node and add a new HTML file to the *partials* folder. Name the new file *login.html*. Replace the content of the newly created file with the code shown here. Notice that we use the ng-submit directive to connect the submit method in our LoginCtrl to the form for form submission:

```
<!-- chapter10/login.html -->

<div class="blog-login-wrapper">

<form class="" ng-submit="submit()" ng-controller="LoginCtrl">
<div class="blog-login-error">{{error}}</div>
<div class="blog-login-label">
<label for="username">Username:</label></div>
<div class="blog-login-element">
<input type="text" ng-model="username" name="username"
  placeholder="username" required/></div>
<div class="blog-login-label">
<label for="password">Password:</label></div>
<div class="blog-login-element">
<input type="password" ng-model="password" name="password"
  placeholder="password" required/></div>
<div class="blog-login-button">
<button type="submit" class="form-button">Sign in</button></div>
</form>

</div>
```

Now open the CSS file *styles.css* in your editor and add the following code to the bottom of the file. Notice that we use CSS3 media queries like @media screen and (min-width: 1200px) to make our login template be responsive and look good on any mobile or desktop platform:

```
/* chapter10/styles.css */

.blog-login-wrapper{
  float: left;
  background: #e0e0e0;
  border-radius:6px;
```

```css
    -moz-border-radius:6px; /* Firefox 3.6 and earlier */
    border: darkgreen solid 1px;
}

@media screen and (min-width: 1200px){
  .blog-login-wrapper{
    width: 40%;
    margin: 10% 0 0 30%;
    padding: 1%;
    background: #e0e0e0;
    border-radius:6px;
    -moz-border-radius:6px; /* Firefox 3.6 and earlier */
    border: darkgreen solid 1px;
  }
}

@media screen and (max-width: 1200px){
  .blog-login-wrapper{
    width: 40%;
    margin: 10% 0 0 30%;
    padding: 1%;
    background: #e0e0e0;
    border-radius:6px;
    -moz-border-radius:6px; /* Firefox 3.6 and earlier */
    border: darkgreen solid 1px;
  }
}

@media screen and (max-width: 600px){
  .blog-login-wrapper{
    width: 80%;
    margin: 10% 0 0 10%;
    padding: 1%;
    background: #e0e0e0;
    border-radius:6px;
    -moz-border-radius:6px; /* Firefox 3.6 and earlier */
    border: darkgreen solid 1px;
  }
}

.blog-login-label{
  float: left;
  width: 70%;
  margin: 0 0 0 15%;
  padding: 1% 0 0 0;
  text-align: center;
}

.blog-login-element{
  float: left;
  width: 70%;
  margin: 0 0 0 15%;
```

```
    padding: 1% 0 0 0;
    text-align: center;
  }

  .blog-login-button{
    float: left;
    width: 100%;
    margin: 0 0 0 0;
    padding: 5% 0 0 0;
    text-align: center;
  }

  .blog-login-error{
    float: left;
    width: 100%;
    margin: 0 0 0 0;
    padding: 0 0 0 0;
    text-align: center;
    color: red;
  }
```

Adding New Routes

Now we need to add the two new routes to our route provider in the *app.js* file. The following code shows the changes needed for this file. As you can see, the two new routes make use of the two new controllers and the new template file:

```
/* chapter10/app.js */

'use strict';
/* App Module */

var blogApp = angular.module('blogApp', [
  'ngRoute',
  'blogControllers',
  'blogServices',
  'blogBusinessServices',
  'blogDirectives'
]);

blogApp.config(['$routeProvider', '$locationProvider',
function($routeProvider, $locationProvider) {
  $routeProvider.
    when('/', {
      templateUrl: 'partials/main.html',
      controller: 'BlogCtrl'
    }).when('/blogPost/:id', {
      templateUrl: 'partials/blogPost.html',
      controller: 'BlogViewCtrl'
    }).when('/login', {
      templateUrl: 'partials/login.html',
```

```
      controller: 'LoginCtrl'
    }).when('/logOut', {
      templateUrl: 'partials/login.html',
      controller: 'LogoutCtrl'
    });

  $locationProvider.html5Mode(false).hashPrefix('!');
}]);
```

Adding a Logout Link

Finally, we need to make one more change to our blog application: we need to modify the *menu.html* file and add the new "Logout" menu link. Here is the line you'll need to add to the *menu.html* file. The new logout link maps to the logout route that we just added:

```
<!-- chapter10/menu.html excerpt -->

<li><a id="lo" href="#!logOut">Logout</a></li>
```

The complete *menu.html* file is shown here for convenience:

```
<!-- chapter10/menu.html complete file -->

<nav class="navbar navbar-inverse navbar-fixed-top" role="navigation">
<!-- Brand and toggle get grouped for better mobile display -->

<div class="container">
<div class="navbar-header">
<button type="button" class="navbar-toggle" data-toggle="collapse"
  data-target=".navbar-collapse">
<span class="sr-only">Toggle navigation</span>
<span class="icon-bar"></span>
<span class="icon-bar"></span>
<span class="icon-bar"></span>
</button>

<a class="navbar-brand" style="{{brandColor}}" href="#!/">{{label}}</a>
</div>

<!--Collect the nav links, forms, and other content for toggling -->
<div class="collapse navbar-collapse">
<ul class="nav navbar-nav">

<li class="{{aboutActiveClass}}"><a href="#!about">About</a></li>
<li class="">
<a href="https://github.com/KenWilliamson">Download Project Code</a>
</li>

<li><a id="lo" href="#!logOut">Logout</a></li>

</ul>
```

```
</div><!-- /.navbar-collapse -->
</div>

</nav>
```

Once you have made all the changes outlined in this chapter, your blog application should have all the needed security additions that were specified. To test the changes that were made, we will run the project and check for errors.

Running the Blog Application

Right-click the project node and select "Run" from the menu. Your project should run and you should see the screen in Figure 10-1. If you do not see the login screen, check that all the changes outlined in this chapter were performed correctly. Turn on developer tools for your browser and look for errors, as described in previous chapters.

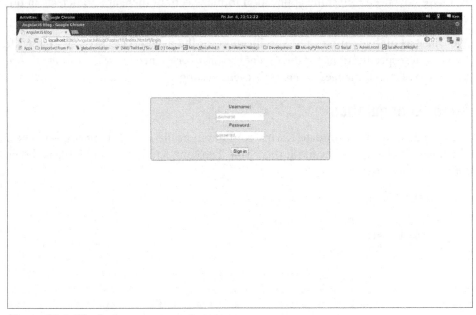

Figure 10-1. The login screen

Logging In

Once your project is running, do the following:

1. Enter "node" as the username.
2. Enter "password" as the password.

3. Click the "Sign in" button.

You should now see the same blog screens that you built in the previous chapters. The application should function just as before with no changes. Navigate through the application to validate that everything works correctly.

If you were to enter incorrect user credentials, you would see the error message described earlier ("Login Failed") displayed in red. Notice the new menu item "Logout" at the right end of the menu bar. Click "Logout" and your session should end. You should then be taken back to the login screen. If the login and logout process work correctly, your security changes were implemented successfully.

Testing with Karma

We've added a new AngularJS service and two new controllers to our blog application. We now need to test the application to make certain there are no defects in our code. We also need to validate that all previous unit tests are still passing.

We will start off by writing a test specification for the new service. We will then write two new test specifications for the two new controllers. Once our unit testing is complete, we will make changes to our end-to-end testing.

Karma Configuration

We already have an up-to-date Karma configuration file for our blog project. There should be no changes to the file at this point. The complete *karma.conf.js* file is shown here for reference:

```
/* chapter10/karma.conf.js */

module.exports = function (config) {
    config.set({
        basePath: '../',
        files: [
            "public_html/js/libs/angular.min.js",
            "public_html/js/libs/angular-mocks.js",
            "public_html/js/libs/angular-route.min.js",
            "public_html/js/libs/angular-resource.min.js",
            "public_html/js/libs/angular-cookies.min.js",
            "public_html/js/*.js",
            "public_html/partials/*.html",
            "test/**/*Spec.js"
        ],
        preprocessors: {
            'public_html/partials/*.html': ['ng-html2js']
        },
        exclude: [
        ],
```

```
            autoWatch: true,
            frameworks: [
                "jasmine"
            ],
            browsers: [
                "Chrome",
                "Firefox"
            ],
            plugins: [
                "karma-junit-reporter",
                "karma-chrome-launcher",
                "karma-firefox-launcher",
                "karma-jasmine",
                "karma-ng-html2js-preprocessor"
            ],
            ngHtml2JsPreprocessor: {
                stripPrefix: 'public_html/'
        });
    };
```

Karma Test Specifications

We need to add unit test specifications for the new Login service and the two new controllers. The following code shows the new test specification for the Login service. The service relies on a REST service, so we will only test to make sure we can inject the service. We will actually test the service interaction with the REST service during end-to-end testing. If there are any issues, we will find them there. Add this test specification to the project's *servicesSpec.js* file:

```
/* chapter10/servicesSpec.js excerpt */

describe('test Login', function () {
  var $rootScope;
  var login;

  beforeEach(module('blogServices'));

  beforeEach(inject(function ($injector) {
    $rootScope = $injector.get('$rootScope');
    login = $injector.get('Login');
  }));

  it('should test Login service', function () {
    expect(login).toBeDefined();
  });
});
```

The complete *servicesSpec.js* file is shown here:

```
/* chapter10/servicesSpec.js complete file */

describe('AngularJS Blog Service Testing', function () {
```

```
describe('test BlogList', function () {
  var $rootScope;
  var blogList;
  beforeEach(module('blogServices'));
  beforeEach(inject(function ($injector) {
    $rootScope = $injector.get('$rootScope');
    blogList = $injector.get('BlogList');
  }));
  it('should test BlogList service', function () {
    expect(blogList).toBeDefined();
  });
});

describe('test BlogPost', function () {
  var $rootScope;
  var blogPost;
  beforeEach(module('blogServices'));
  beforeEach(inject(function ($injector) {
    $rootScope = $injector.get('$rootScope');
    blogPost = $injector.get('BlogPost');
  }));
  it('should test BlogPost service', function () {
    expect(blogPost).toBeDefined();
  });
});

describe('test Login', function () {
  var $rootScope;
   var login;
  beforeEach(module('blogServices'));
  beforeEach(inject(function ($injector) {
    $rootScope = $injector.get('$rootScope');
    login = $injector.get('Login');
  }));
  it('should test Login service', function () {
    expect(login).toBeDefined();
  });
});
});
```

Now we need test specifications for the two new controllers. First we show the test specification for the `LoginCtrl` controller. We first get a reference to the controller and then call the `submit` method attached to the scope. We use a scope property to validate that the method call was successful:

```
/* chapter10/controllerSpec.js excerpt */

describe('LoginCtrl', function () {
    var scope, ctrl;

    beforeEach(inject(function ($rootScope, $controller) {
        scope = $rootScope.$new();
```

```
        ctrl = $controller('LoginCtrl', {$scope: scope});
        scope.submit();
    }));
    it('should show submit success', function () {
        console.log("LoginCtrl:" + scope.sub);
        expect(scope.sub).toEqual(true);
    });
});
```

Next is the test specification for the `LogoutCtrl` controller. In this case, we just validate that we can get a reference to the controller. We will validate that the controller actually handles logout correctly when we do end-to-end testing:

```
/* chapter10/controllerSpec.js excerpt */

describe('LogoutCtrl', function () {
        var scope, ctrl;

        beforeEach(inject(function ($rootScope, $controller) {
            scope = $rootScope.$new();
            ctrl = $controller('LogoutCtrl', {$scope: scope});
        }));

        it('should create LogoutCtrl controller', function () {
            console.log("LogoutCtrl:" + ctrl);
            expect(ctrl).toBeDefined();
            //expect(scope.blogList).toBeUndefined();
        });
    });
```

The complete *controllerSpec.js* file is shown next. Make the changes to your file in the blog application and validate that it matches the version shown here:

```
/* chapter10/controllerSpec.js complete file */

describe('AngularJS Blog Application', function () {
  beforeEach(module('blogApp'));
  //beforeEach(module('blogServices'));

  describe('BlogCtrl', function () {
    var scope, ctrl;
    beforeEach(inject(function ($rootScope, $controller) {
      scope = $rootScope.$new();
      ctrl = $controller('BlogCtrl', {$scope: scope});
    }));
    it('should create show blog entry count', function () {
      console.log("blogList:" + scope.blogList);
      expect(scope.blogList.length).toEqual(0);
      //expect(scope.blogList).toBeUndefined();
    });
  });
```

```
describe('BlogViewCtrl', function () {
  var scope, ctrl, $httpBackend;
  beforeEach(inject(function (_$httpBackend_, $routeParams,
    $rootScope, $controller) {
    $httpBackend = _$httpBackend_;
    $httpBackend.expectGET('blogPost').respond({_id: '1'});
    $routeParams.id = '1';
    scope = $rootScope.$new();
    ctrl = $controller('BlogViewCtrl', {$scope: scope});
  }));
  it('should show blog entry id', function () {
    //expect(scope.blogEntry._id).toEqual(1);
    //expect(scope.blogList).toBeUndefined();
    expect(scope.blg).toEqual(1);
  });

});

describe('LoginCtrl', function () {
  var scope, ctrl;
  beforeEach(inject(function ($rootScope, $controller) {
    scope = $rootScope.$new();
    ctrl = $controller('LoginCtrl', {$scope: scope});
    scope.submit();
  }));
  it('should show submit success', function () {
    console.log("LoginCtrl:" + scope.sub);
    expect(scope.sub).toEqual(true);
    //expect(scope.blogList).toBeUndefined();
  });
});

describe('LogoutCtrl', function () {
  var scope, ctrl;
  beforeEach(inject(function ($rootScope, $controller) {
    scope = $rootScope.$new();
    ctrl = $controller('LogoutCtrl', {$scope: scope});
  }));
  it('should create LogoutCtrl controller', function () {
    console.log("LogoutCtrl:" + ctrl);
    expect(ctrl).toBeDefined();
    //expect(scope.blogList).toBeUndefined();
  });
});
});
```

Karma Testing

The test specifications just added will test the new service and the two new controllers. We will also test all the existing controllers, the existing services, and the existing
directive when Karma runs.

Right-click the project and select "Test" from the menu. Karma will start. You should see both Chrome and Firefox browser windows open. The NetBeans test results window should open and display a total of 26 passed test cases.

If you get any error messages or failed tests, go back over this section and verify that you completed all the configurations and installations. You can also download the Chapter 10 code from the GitHub project site (*https://github.com/KenWilliamson*).

End-to-End Testing

We will make several changes to the end-to-end test specifications for our blog application here. We will need to log into the blog application with the script. Then, once logged in, we will navigate through the blog as before to verify that all previous E2E functionality still works. We will then need to log out with the test script to test the logout functionality.

Protractor Configuration

We already created a Protractor configuration file for the blog application in Chapter 5. The Protractor configuration file is shown here for reference:

```
/* chapter10/conf.js Protractor configuration file */

exports.config = {
  seleniumAddress: 'http://localhost:4444/wd/hub',
  specs: ['e2e/blog-spec.js']
};
```

Protractor Test Specification

The *blog-spec.js* file shown here contains several changes. First notice that the script needs to complete the login form by populating the username and password fields. Then it looks up the login form button by the CSS class name, and clicks the button:

```
/* chapter10/blog-spec.js Protractor test specification */

describe("Blog Application Test", function(){
  it("should test the main blog page", function(){
    browser.get("http://localhost:8383/AngularJsBlog/");
    //logs into the blog application
    element(by.model("username")).sendKeys("node");
    element(by.model("password")).sendKeys("password");
    element(by.css('.form-button')).click();
    expect(browser.getTitle()).toEqual("AngularJS Blog");
    //gets the blog list
    var blogList =
      element.all(by.repeater('blogPost in blogList'));
    //tests the size of the blogList
    expect(blogList.count()).toEqual(1);
```

```
browser.get(
  "http://localhost:8383/AngularJsBlog/#!/
  blogPost/5394e59c4f50850000e6b7ea");
expect(browser.getTitle()).toEqual("AngularJS Blog");

//gets the comment list
var commentList =
  element.all(by.repeater('comment in blogEntry.comments'));
  //checks the size of the commentList
  expect(commentList.count()).toEqual(2);
  element(by.css('.navbar-brand')).click();
  //logs out of the blog application
  element(by.id('lo')).click();
  expect(browser.getTitle()).toEqual("AngularJS Blog");
});
});
```

Once the script has successfully logged into the application, it navigates through the application as before. Then, at the end of the test script, it looks up the logout link by id. It then clicks the link, logging out of the application.

The end-to-end test specification validates that the login process works. It also validates all the previous functionality tested in Chapter 9. Then it validates that the logout process works correctly.

Protractor Testing

Now, with those changes added, we are ready to start the end-to-end testing.

Start a new command window and enter the following command to start the test server:

```
webdriver-manager start
```

Open a new command window and navigate to the root of the Chapter 10 project. Type the command:

```
protractor test/conf.js
```

You should see a browser window open. You should then see the test script log into the blog application and navigate through the pages of the application, and finally log out of the application. When the Protractor script has finished, the browser window will close.

You should see results like the following in the command window when the Protractor script completes. The number of seconds that it takes the script to finish will vary depending on your particular system:

```
Finished in 3.285 seconds
1 test, 5 assertions, 0 failures
```

One Last Point on Security

I want to emphasize one last thing about implementing security in a JavaScript application. Any security that you implement in JavaScript can be circumvented by the user, as I explained at the start of the chapter. The login screen and security that we implemented in this chapter are completely dependent on the login REST service.

The login screen is used just as a way to gather and store the user's credentials in a safe place temporarily and to control the authentication process for each REST service that contains private data. The user's credentials are removed after each session and have to be entered again at each login, unless the user chooses to save their credentials.

Conclusion

In the next chapter you will see how the user's credentials are used to gain access to private REST services that add new blog posts and comments. You will first deploy the REST services and the AngularJS application together in a MEAN stack deployment to your local machine to see the whole process in action. Once the application is up and running on your local machine, you will be able to use the developer tools in Chrome to view the REST service logs at runtime: you'll be able to view the URL, request, and response of each service call.

You will also see any errors that occur. Once you have tested the MEAN stack on your local machine, you will deploy the project to the cloud using Git, which is a distributed version control and source code management (SCM) system initially developed by Linus Torvalds.

MEAN Cloud and Mobile

This chapter will cover both the cloud deployment of our blog application and a short discussion on building a mobile HTML5 version of our application. The cloud deployment will be to a free account on RedHat's OpenShift platform. The mobile discussion will cover the steps needed to build a mobile version of the blog application that will run on any mobile device and can be distributed through the respective mobile application stores. The mobile version will use the same REST services that we use for the cloud version of our blog application.

Local Deployment

Before we deploy our blog application to the cloud, we will set up a local project in NetBeans that we will later use to deploy our blog to OpenShift. We can also run and test our blog application locally before pushing it to the cloud. All the code for this chapter has already been written and can be downloaded from GitHub (*http://bit.ly/lajs-github*). We will walk through the code and discuss the changes that have been made to our AngularJS application to allow for a deployment to the cloud.

Our cloud deployment uses Node.js as the server platform, ExpressJS as the web application framework, and MongoDB as the database. We will discuss how AngularJS integrates with all three of these to form a MEAN (MongoDB, ExpressJS, AngularJS, and Node.js) stack deployment. We will primarily focus on the role that AngularJS plays in a MEAN stack application.

We will not cover the Node.js code in great detail. Although the Node.js server-side code is JavaScript, it can often be quite complex. If you have server-side experience, feel free to experiment with the server code. Books written specifically on the MEAN stack will cover the Node.js and ExpressJS code of MEAN stack applications in much greater depth than we will here.

Installing Node.js, npm, and MongoDB

Before you can run the new MEAN blog application locally, you must install Node.js, MongoDB, and npm (the Node.js package manager) on your local system. The installations are different for each operating system, but you can find more information about Node.js at *nodejs.org* and you can find information about MongoDB at *http://www.mongodb.org*. If you are using one of the Linux distributions, you can usually install and configure both Node.js and MongoDB through the OS package management system. Before we continue, install and configure Node.js, npm, and MongoDB if you haven't done so already.

Installing the NetBeans Node.js Plugin

Now we will install a Node.js plugin for NetBeans to simplify our interaction with Node.js. Do the following:

1. Follow the directions on Tim Boudreau's blog (*http://bit.ly/tb-nodejs*).
2. Download and install the plugin.
3. Configure the plugin as specified.

Once you have the Node.js plugin for NetBeans installed and configured, download the source for this chapter from GitHub (*http://bit.ly/nodemeanblog*). Unzip the file somewhere on your local drive. In NetBeans, click "File" and select "Open Project" from the menu, then navigate to the project source that you just downloaded and open the Node.js project. You should see the NodeBlog project, as shown in Figure 11-1.

Figure 11-1. The NodeBlog project in NetBeans

The MEAN Application

We'll use MongoDB as our server-side database. MongoDB is a NoSQL database that is fast and easy to use. With MongoDB, there is no concern about writing SQL queries; we just use the MongoDB API to interact with the database. We'll actually simplify our interaction with MongoDB even more by using Mongoose.js (*http://mongoosejs.com/*), an object data modeling (ODM) library that allows us to interact with MongoDB using JSON via a greatly simplified API interface.

Our MEAN stack uses REST services built with ExpressJS (*http://expressjs.com/*). ExpressJS is a web framework that is lightweight and easy to use. REST services built on ExpressJS can be used exclusively in our application or exposed to the outside world for use by external applications.

MEAN stack applications run on Node.js, which runs on Google's V8 JavaScript engine. Node.js is a very powerful platform for developing server-side software applications in JavaScript. AngularJS sits on top of the other three pieces of the MEAN stack and is used to build JavaScript applications that interact directly with the REST services built with ExpressJS.

Node.js Public Folder

You will notice our AngularJS blog code is now located under the *public* folder in the MEAN project. Placing the AngularJS code in the *public* folder is common practice when you're building MEAN applications. Open the *public* folder and you should see the same code that we developed in the previous chapters.

MEAN Services

Several changes were needed to our *services.js* file, as shown in the following code. Notice that we changed the URL for each service from *http://nodeblog-micbuttoncloud.rhcloud.com/NodeBlog/* to *./NodeBlog/*. That small change makes our application transportable to any cloud platform. Without making that change, we would need to configure the service URLs every time we moved the application to a new cloud platform:

```
/* chapter11/services.js */

'use strict';
/* Services */

var blogServices =
angular.module('blogServices', ['ngResource']);

blogServices.factory('BlogPost', ['$resource',
  function($resource) {
```

```
      return $resource("./NodeBlog/blog/:id", {}, {
        get: {method: 'GET', cache: false, isArray: false},
        save: {method: 'POST', cache: false, isArray: false},
        update: {method: 'PUT', cache: false, isArray: false},
        delete: {method: 'DELETE', cache: false, isArray: false}
      });
}]);

blogServices.factory('BlogList', ['$resource',
  function($resource) {
    return $resource("./NodeBlog/blogList", {}, {
      get: {method: 'GET', cache: false, isArray: true}
    });
}]);

blogServices.factory('Login', ['$resource',
  function($resource) {
    return $resource("./NodeBlog/login", {}, {
      login: {method: 'POST', cache: false, isArray: false}
    });
}]);

blogServices.factory('BlogPostComments', ['$resource',
  function($resource) {
    return $resource("./NodeBlog/comment/:id", {}, {
      save: {method: 'POST', cache: false, isArray: false}
    });
}]);
```

We also made changes to the application to allow the user to create new blog posts
and to add comments to posts. One of those changes was to this file as well: notice
that we added a new BlogPostComments service at the bottom of the file. There were
also changes made to other files in the application. We will first discuss the changes to
controllers.js.

MEAN Blog Controllers

Following is the new *controllers.js* file, which we've modified to give us the ability to
add new blog posts and comments. Notice first the changes that were made to the
BlogViewCtrl controller. We've injected several new services into the controller,
including the BlogPostComments service just shown. We've also added a new submit
method to the controller that handles the process of adding a new comment to a blog
post. The new submit method makes a call to the save method on the BlogPostCom
ments service:

```
/* chapter11/controllers.js */

'use strict';
/* Controllers */
```

```
var blogControllers =
  angular.module('blogControllers', []);

blogControllers.controller('BlogCtrl',
  ['$scope', 'BlogList', '$location', 'checkCreds',
    function BlogCtrl($scope, BlogList, $location, checkCreds) {
      if (!checkCreds()) {
        $location.path('/login');
      }
      $scope.brandColor = "color: white;";
      $scope.blogList = [];
      BlogList.get({},
        function success(response) {
          console.log("Success:" + JSON.stringify(response));
          $scope.blogList = response;
        },
        function error(errorResponse) {
          console.log("Error:" + JSON.stringify(errorResponse));
      });
}]);

blogControllers.controller('BlogViewCtrl',
  ['$scope', '$routeParams', 'BlogPost', 'BlogPostComments',
    '$location', 'checkCreds', '$http', 'getToken', '$route',
    function BlogViewCtrl($scope, $routeParams, BlogPost,
      BlogPostComments, $location, checkCreds, $http, getToken,
        $route) {
      if (!checkCreds()) {
        $location.path('/login');
      }
      var blogId = $routeParams.id;
      $scope.blg = 1;

      BlogPost.get({id: blogId},
        function success(response) {
          console.log("Success:" + JSON.stringify(response));
          $scope.blogEntry = response;
          $scope.blogId = response._id;
        },
        function error(errorResponse) {
          console.log("Error:" + JSON.stringify(errorResponse));
        }
    );

    $scope.submit = function() {
    $scope.sub = true;
    $http.defaults.headers.common['Authorization'] = 'Basic ' +
      getToken();
    var postData = {
      "commentText": $scope.commentText,
      "blog" : $scope.blogId
```

```
      };

    BlogPostComments.save({}, postData,
      function success(response) {
        console.log("Success:" + JSON.stringify(response));
        $location.path('/blogPost/'+$scope.blogId);
        $route.reload();
      },
      function error(errorResponse) {
        console.log("Error:" + JSON.stringify(errorResponse));
      });
    };
}]);

blogControllers.controller('LoginCtrl', ['$scope',
  '$location', 'Login', 'setCreds',
    function LoginCtrl($scope, $location, Login, setCreds) {
      $scope.submit = function() {
      $scope.sub = true;
      var postData = {
        "username": $scope.username,
        "password": $scope.password
      };
      Login.login({}, postData,
        function success(response) {
          console.log("Success:" + JSON.stringify(response));
          if (response.authenticated) {
            setCreds($scope.username, $scope.password)
            $location.path('/');
          } else {
            $scope.error = "Login Failed"
          }
        },
        function error(errorResponse) {
          console.log("Error:" + JSON.stringify(errorResponse));
        });
    };
}]);


blogControllers.controller('LogoutCtrl', ['$location', 'deleteCreds',
    function LogoutCtrl($location, deleteCreds) {
      deleteCreds();
      $location.path('/login');
}]);


blogControllers.controller('NewBlogPostCtrl',
  ['$scope', 'BlogPost', '$location', 'checkCreds', '$http', 'getToken',
    function NewBlogPostCtrl($scope, BlogPost, $location, checkCreds,
      $http, getToken) {
      if (!checkCreds()) {
```

```
        $location.path('/login');
      }
      $scope.languageList = [
        {
          "id": 1,
          "name" : "English"
        },
        {
          "id": 2,
          "name" : "Spanish"
        }
      ];
      $scope.languageId = 1;
      $scope.newActiveClass = "active";
      $scope.submit = function() {
      $scope.sub = true;
      $http.defaults.headers.common['Authorization'] = 'Basic ' +
        getToken();
      var postData = {
        "introText": $scope.introText,
        "blogText" : $scope.blogText,
        "languageId": $scope.languageId
      };

      BlogPost.save({}, postData,
        function success(response) {
          console.log("Success:" + JSON.stringify(response));
          $location.path('/');
        },
        function error(errorResponse) {
          console.log("Error:" + JSON.stringify(errorResponse));
        });
      };
  }]);


blogControllers.controller('AboutBlogCtrl', ['$scope',
  '$location', 'checkCreds',
    function AboutBlogCtrl($scope, $location, checkCreds) {
      if (!checkCreds()) {
        $location.path('/login');
      }
      $scope.aboutActiveClass = "active";
}]);
```

The REST service linked to the BlogPostComments service requires Basic Authentication. If you look at the first line of the new submit method added to the Blog ViewCtrl controller ($http.defaults.headers.common['Authorization'] = 'Basic' + getToken();), you will see how REST service Basic Authentication is handled in AngularJS. The code on that line makes use of the `$http` service to add a Basic Authentication header to the REST service call.

We use the `getToken` AngularJS business logic service developed in Chapter 8 to add the base64 token to the header, as described in that chapter. Once a new comment is added successfully, we then make a call to the `path` method on the `$location` service (`$location.path('/blogPost/'+$scope.blogId);`) and a call to the `reload` method on the `$route` service (`$route.reload();`). Making those two calls refreshes the blog post page to show the newly added comment.

We also added a new controller named `NewBlogPostCtrl`. The new controller has a `submit` method that makes a call to the `BlogPost` service used previously. The `save` method is called on the `BlogPost` service, and the REST service mapped to the `save` method requires Basic Authentication, as described previously. The implementation for authentication is the same.

MEAN Blog Templates

The new controller also has a new `languageList` JSON array that is used to populate a new HTML `<select>` element in the template used for new blog posts. The language field is not actually used by our blog application but is included to show how to populate a `<select>` element in an AngularJS view. We preselect the `<select>` element with "English" by setting the `languageId` scope property (`$scope.languageId = 1;`).

There were no other significant changes made to the *controllers.js* file. We will now talk about the new template added to allow users to add new blog posts. We will also cover changes made to the blog post template needed for adding comments to blog entries.

Adding Comments

The following code shows the modifications needed to the existing blog post template. You will notice that we've added a new form for submitting new comments. The new form is mapped to the new `submit` method of the `BlogEntryCtrl` controller. Also notice that we hold the blog ID in a hidden element and pass that ID back to the controller when the user submits the form. The blog ID is passed to the REST service that adds new comments:

```
<!-- chapter11/blogPost.html -->

<div blg-menu menu-title="AngularJS MEAN Blog"></div>
<div id="container" class="container">
<div class="blog-post-label">Blog Entry</div>
<div class="blog-entry-wrapper">
```

```
<div class="blog-intro-text">
Posted: {{blogEntry.date| date:'MM/dd/yyyy @ h:mma'}}
</div>
<div class="blog-entry-outer">
{{blogEntry.blogText}}
</div>
<div class="blog-comment-wrapper">
<div class="blog-comment-label">Blog Comments</div>
<div class="blog-entry-comments" ng-repeat="comment in blogEntry.comments">
{{comment.commentText}}
</div>
</div>

<div class="blog-comment-entry-wrapper">

<form class="" ng-submit="submit()" ng-controller="BlogViewCtrl">

<input type="hidden" ng-model="blogId"/>
<div class="blog-post-entry-label">
<label for="commentText">New Comment:</label>
</div>
<div class="blog-post-entry-element">
<textarea class="blog-post-textarea" type="text"
ng-model="commentText" name="commentText" placeholder="Comment" required/>
</div>
<div class="blog-post-button">
<button type="submit" class="form-button">Submit</button>
</div>

</form>

</div>

</div>
</div>
```

Adding Blog Entries

The following code shows the new template used to add new blog posts. The template maps form submission to the submit method of the NewBlogPostCtrl controller using the ng-submit directive, as before:

```
<!-- chapter11/newPost.html -->

<div blg-menu menu-title="AngularJS MEAN Blog"></div>
<div id="container" class="container">
<div class="blog-post-label">New Blog Posts</div>
<div class="blog-post-wrapper">
```

```
<form class="" ng-submit="submit()" ng-controller="NewBlogPostCtrl">

<div class="blog-post-entry-label">
<label for="introText">Intro Text:</label></div>
<div class="blog-post-entry-element">
<textarea class="blog-post-textarea" type="text"
ng-model="introText" name="introText" placeholder="Intro Text"  required/></div>

<div class="blog-post-entry-label">
<label for="blogText">Blog Text:</label></div>
<div class="blog-post-entry-element">
<textarea class="blog-post-textarea" type="text"
ng-model="blogText" name="blogText" placeholder="Blog Text"  required/></div>

<div class="blog-post-entry-label">
<label for="blogText">Language:</label></div>
<div class="blog-post-entry-element">
<select class="form-select-element-left" ng-model="languageId"
ng-options="lan.id as lan.name for lan in languageList"
name="languageId" required>
</select>
</div>

<div class="blog-post-button"><button type="submit"
class="form-button">Submit</button></div>

</form>
</div>
</div>
```

The following code shows the change needed to the *menu.html* file: we've added a link in the menu to the new blog post creation view. The new path configuration is also shown:

```
<!-- chapter11/menu.html -->

<nav class="navbar navbar-inverse navbar-fixed-top" role="navigation">
<!-- Brand and toggle get grouped for better mobile display -->
<div class="container">
<div class="navbar-header">
<button type="button" class="navbar-toggle" data-toggle="collapse"
  data-target=".navbar-collapse">
<span class="sr-only">Toggle navigation</span>
<span class="icon-bar"></span>
<span class="icon-bar"></span>
<span class="icon-bar"></span>
</button>
<a class="navbar-brand" style="{{brandColor}}" href="#!/">{{label}}</a>
</div>

<!--Collect the nav links, forms, and other content for toggling -->
```

```
<div class="collapse navbar-collapse">
<ul class="nav navbar-nav">
<li class="{{aboutActiveClass}}"><a href="#!about">About</a></li>

<li class="{{newActiveClass}}"><a href="#!newBlogPost">New</a></li>

<li class="">
<a href="https://github.com/KenWilliamson">Download Project Code</a>
</li>
<li><a href="#!logOut">Logout</a></li>
</ul>

</div><!-- /.navbar-collapse -->
</div>

</nav>
```

Adding New Routes

The following code shows the changes needed for the *app.js* file. The new route used to add a new blog post is shown. The route was added to the $routeProvider as before:

```
/* chapter11/app.js excerpt */

.when('/newBlogPost', {
  templateUrl: 'partials/newPost.html',
  controller: 'NewBlogPostCtrl'
})
```

The complete *app.js* file is shown here for convenience:

```
/* chapter11/app.js complete file */

'use strict';
/* App Module */

var blogApp = angular.module('blogApp', [
  'ngRoute',
  'blogControllers',
  'blogServices',
  'blogBusinessServices',
  'blogDirectives'
]);

blogApp.config(['$routeProvider', '$locationProvider',
  function($routeProvider, $locationProvider) {
    $routeProvider.
    when('/', {
      templateUrl: 'partials/main.html',
      controller: 'BlogCtrl'
```

```
    }).when('/blogPost/:id', {
      templateUrl: 'partials/blogPost.html',
      controller: 'BlogViewCtrl'
    }).when('/newBlogPost', {
      templateUrl: 'partials/newPost.html',
      controller: 'NewBlogPostCtrl'
    }).when('/about', {
      templateUrl: 'partials/about.html',
      controller: 'AboutBlogCtrl'
    }).when('/login', {
      templateUrl: 'partials/login.html',
      controller: 'LoginCtrl'
    }).when('/logOut', {
      templateUrl: 'partials/login.html',
      controller: 'LogoutCtrl'
    });
    $locationProvider.html5Mode(false).hashPrefix('!');
}]);
```

Adding Node.js Dependencies

No other significant changes were made to the blog application. We will now run the application locally before deploying to the cloud.

There is one small command-line task that needs to be performed before you can run the blog application locally. This is standard practice when working with Node.js. Do the following:

1. Open a command window and navigate to the location on your drive where you unzipped the NodeBlog project.

2. You should see the *package.json* file at that location.

3. In the command window, do the following:
   a. Type **npm install**.
   b. Press Enter.

This command uses npm to install all the blog application dependencies. If the installation was successful, you should see all the required Node.js packages installed in the current directory under a new folder named *node_modules*.

When you run the **npm install** command, npm reads the *package.json* file and installs all the required packages that are defined in that file. If there were errors and the new folder didn't get created, there is a problem with the Node.js installation on your machine. Once you have the required Node.js packages installed in your project, you are ready to run the project.

Running the Blog Application Locally

Right-click the NodeBlog project and select "Run" from the menu. You should see a small indicator at the bottom right of NetBeans, as shown in Figure 11-2. If you see "Running," your project and Node.js are installed correctly. Open a browser and navigate to *http://localhost:8080*, and you should see the login screen as before.

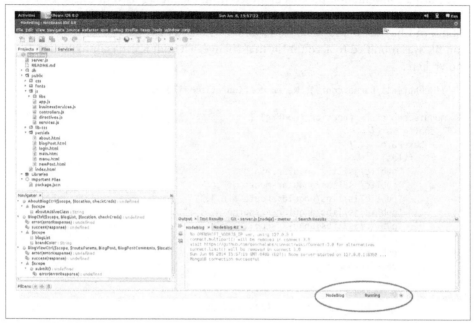

Figure 11-2. Running the NodeBlog project

Log in with the following credentials:

- username = "node"
- password = "password"

The application should perform just as it did before. If you have any issues running the application locally, resolve those issues before you continue. Once the application runs locally on your machine, continue on to the next section.

Testing with Karma

We've added a new `BlogPostComments` service to the *services.js* file, and made changes to the *controllers.js* file. In order to validate that everything is working correctly, we need to update the test specifications as well. If you look at the test specifications for controllers and services in the downloaded code for this chapter, you will see the needed changes and additions.

First I will show how to configure Karma in a MEAN stack environment. Then we will look at the test specification for the new BlogPostComments service and the changes to the test specifications for controllers.

Karma Configuration

The Karma configuration file was modified from the file we used in Chapter 10. Now the AngularJS application is located under the *public* folder of the MEAN blog application. In Chapter 10, the *public_html* folder was used instead. The Karma configuration file was modified to account for that change. The full Karma configuration file is shown here:

```
/* chapter11/karma.conf.js Karma configuration file */

module.exports = function (config) {
  config.set({
    basePath: '../',
      files: [
        "public/js/libs/angular.min.js",
        "public/js/libs/angular-mocks.js",
        "public/js/libs/angular-route.min.js",
        "public/js/libs/angular-resource.min.js",
        "public/js/libs/angular-cookies.min.js",
        "public/js/*.js",
        "public/partials/*.html",
        "test/**/*Spec.js"
      ],
    preprocessors: {
      'public/partials/*.html': ['ng-html2js']
    },
    exclude: [
    ],
    autoWatch: true,
    frameworks: [
      "jasmine"
    ],
    browsers: [
      "Chrome",
      "Firefox"
    ],
    plugins: [
      "karma-junit-reporter",
      "karma-chrome-launcher",
      "karma-firefox-launcher",
      "karma-jasmine",
      "karma-ng-html2js-preprocessor"
    ],
    ngHtml2JsPreprocessor: {
      stripPrefix: 'public/'
    }
```

```
      });
    };
```

There is one other thing to note if you are using NetBeans: a Node.js project in Net-Beans does not have built-in support for Karma. That is not really a problem; we just need to launch Karma from the command line instead. We will cover that in the next section.

Now, before we start unit testing, we need to install all the Node.js dependencies defined in the project's *package.json* file. Do the following:

1. Navigate to the location where you unzipped the MEAN blog project.

2. Navigate to the location of the *package.json* file.

3. Type the following command to install all dependencies:

```
npm install
```

The install process will run for several minutes. When all packages are installed, you will be ready to move on to the next section.

Karma Test Specifications

The test specification for the new `BlogPostComments` service is shown next. We will only verify that we can inject the service at this point. We will completely check the service when we do E2E testing:

```
/* chapter11/servicesSpec.js excerpt */

describe('test BlogPostComments', function () {
  var $rootScope;
  var comment;
  beforeEach(module('blogServices'));
  beforeEach(inject(function ($injector) {
    $rootScope = $injector.get('$rootScope');
    comment = $injector.get('BlogPostComments');
  }));
  it('should test BlogPostComments service', function () {
    expect(comment).toBeDefined();
  });
});
```

The new test specification for the `NewBlogPostCtrl` controller is shown next. Notice that we make a call to the `submit` method that is attached to the controller's scope. We then validate that the call to the `submit` method was successful:

```
/* chapter11/controllerSpec.js excerpt */

describe('NewBlogPostCtrl', function () {
  var scope, ctrl;
  beforeEach(inject(function ($rootScope, $controller) {
```

```
    scope = $rootScope.$new();
    ctrl = $controller('NewBlogPostCtrl', {$scope: scope});
    scope.submit();
  }));
  it('should show submit success of NewBlogPostCtrl',
    function () {
      console.log("NewBlogPostCtrl:" + scope.sub);
      expect(scope.sub).toEqual(true);
    });
});
```

Next up is the test specification for the `AboutBlogCtrl` controller. We validate the functionality of the controller by checking the value assigned to the `aboutActive Class` variable:

```
/* chapter11/controllerSpec.js excerpt */

describe('AboutBlogCtrl', function () {
  var scope, ctrl;
  beforeEach(inject(function ($rootScope, $controller) {
    scope = $rootScope.$new();
    ctrl = $controller('AboutBlogCtrl', {$scope: scope});
  }));
  it('should create AboutBlogCtrl controller', function () {
    console.log("AboutBlogCtrl:" + ctrl);
    expect(scope.aboutActiveClass).toEqual("active");
  });
});
```

We also made a change to the test specification for the `BlogViewCtrl` controller, as shown here. We now need to validate a call to the new `submit` method attached to the scope of that controller:

```
/* chapter11/controllerSpec.js  excerpt */

describe('BlogViewCtrl', function () {
  var scope, ctrl, $httpBackend;
  beforeEach(inject(function (_$httpBackend_,
    $routeParams, $rootScope, $controller) {
      $httpBackend = _$httpBackend_;
      $httpBackend.expectGET('blogPost').respond({_id: '1'});
      $routeParams.id = '1';
      scope = $rootScope.$new();
      ctrl = $controller('BlogViewCtrl', {$scope: scope});
      scope.submit();
    }));
  it('should show blog entry id', function () {
    expect(scope.blg).toEqual(1);
    expect(scope.sub).toEqual(true);
  });
});
```

The complete *servicesSpec.js* and *controllerSpec.js* files are shown next for reference:

```
/* chapter11/servicesSpec.js complete file */

describe('AngularJS Blog Service Testing', function () {
  describe('test BlogList', function () {
    var $rootScope;
    var blogList;

    beforeEach(module('blogServices'));

    beforeEach(inject(function ($injector) {
      $rootScope = $injector.get('$rootScope');
      blogList = $injector.get('BlogList');
    }));

    it('should test BlogList service', function () {
      expect(blogList).toBeDefined();
    });

  });

  describe('test BlogPost', function () {
    var $rootScope;
    var blogPost;

    beforeEach(module('blogServices'));

    beforeEach(inject(function ($injector) {
      $rootScope = $injector.get('$rootScope');
      blogPost = $injector.get('BlogPost');
    }));

    it('should test BlogPost service', function () {
      expect(blogPost).toBeDefined();
    });
  });

  describe('test Login', function () {
    var $rootScope;
    var login;

    beforeEach(module('blogServices'));

    beforeEach(inject(function ($injector) {
      $rootScope = $injector.get('$rootScope');
      login = $injector.get('Login');
    }));

    it('should test Login service', function () {
      expect(login).toBeDefined();
    });
  });
```

```
  describe('test BlogPostComments', function () {
    var $rootScope;
    var comment;

    beforeEach(module('blogServices'));

    beforeEach(inject(function ($injector) {
      $rootScope = $injector.get('$rootScope');
      comment = $injector.get('BlogPostComments');
    }));

    it('should test BlogPostComments service', function () {
      expect(comment).toBeDefined();
    });
  });
});

/* chapter11/controllerSpec.js complete file */

describe('AngularJS Blog Application', function () {
    beforeEach(module('blogApp'));
    //beforeEach(module('blogServices'));

    describe('BlogCtrl', function () {
      var scope, ctrl;
      beforeEach(inject(function ($rootScope, $controller) {
        scope = $rootScope.$new();
        ctrl = $controller('BlogCtrl', {$scope: scope});
      }));
      it('should create show blog entry count', function () {
        console.log("blogList:" + scope.blogList);
        expect(scope.blogList.length).toEqual(0);
        //expect(scope.blogList).toBeUndefined();
      });
    });

    describe('BlogViewCtrl', function () {
      var scope, ctrl, $httpBackend;
      beforeEach(inject(function (_$httpBackend_, $routeParams,
      $rootScope, $controller) {
        $httpBackend = _$httpBackend_;
        $httpBackend.expectGET('blogPost').respond({_id: '1'});
        $routeParams.id = '1';
        scope = $rootScope.$new();
        ctrl = $controller('BlogViewCtrl', {$scope: scope});
        scope.submit();
      }));

      it('should show blog entry id', function () {
        //expect(scope.blogEntry._id).toEqual(1);
        //expect(scope.blogList).toBeUndefined();
        expect(scope.blg).toEqual(1);
```

```
      expect(scope.sub).toEqual(true);
    });
  });

  describe('LoginCtrl', function () {
    var scope, ctrl;
    beforeEach(inject(function ($rootScope, $controller) {
      scope = $rootScope.$new();
      ctrl = $controller('LoginCtrl', {$scope: scope});
      scope.submit();
    }));
    it('should show submit success', function () {
      console.log("LoginCtrl:" + scope.sub);
      expect(scope.sub).toEqual(true);
      //expect(scope.blogList).toBeUndefined();
    });
  });

  describe('LogoutCtrl', function () {
    var scope, ctrl;
    beforeEach(inject(function ($rootScope, $controller) {
      scope = $rootScope.$new();
      ctrl = $controller('LogoutCtrl', {$scope: scope});
    }));

    it('should create LogoutCtrl controller', function () {
      console.log("LogoutCtrl:" + ctrl);
      expect(ctrl).toBeDefined();
      //expect(scope.blogList).toBeUndefined();
    });
  });

  describe('NewBlogPostCtrl', function () {
    var scope, ctrl;
    beforeEach(inject(function ($rootScope, $controller) {
      scope = $rootScope.$new();
      ctrl = $controller('NewBlogPostCtrl', {$scope: scope});
      scope.submit();
    }));

    it('should show submit success of NewBlogPostCtrl',
      function () {
        console.log("NewBlogPostCtrl:" + scope.sub);
        expect(scope.sub).toEqual(true);
        //expect(scope.blogList).toBeUndefined();
      });
  });

  describe('AboutBlogCtrl', function () {
    var scope, ctrl;
    beforeEach(inject(function ($rootScope, $controller) {
      scope = $rootScope.$new();
```

```
        ctrl = $controller('AboutBlogCtrl', {$scope: scope});
      }));

      it('should create AboutBlogCtrl controller', function () {
        console.log("AboutBlogCtrl:" + ctrl);
        expect(scope.aboutActiveClass).toEqual("active");
        //expect(scope.blogList).toBeUndefined();
      });
    });
  });
```

Karma Testing

Now we need to launch Karma and verify that all tests were successful. We need to use the command line to launch Karma, as mentioned earlier. Do the following:

1. Open a command window.

2. Navigate to the location of the MEAN blog project.

3. Navigate inside the project to where the *test* folder and the *package.json* file are located.

4. Type this command to launch Karma:

```
karma start test/karma.conf.js
```

You should see a Chrome and a Firefox browser window open. You should then see text like the following displayed in the command window, indicating success:

```
Chrome 38.0.2125 (Linux): Executed 16 of 16 SUCCESS (0.17 secs)
Firefox 33.0.0 (Ubuntu): Executed 16 of 16 SUCCESS (0.157 secs)
TOTAL: 32 SUCCESS
```

End-to-End Testing

The MEAN blog application requires a change to the URL in the E2E test specifications. As in Chapter 10, the script will need to log into the blog application. Then, once logged in, it will navigate through the blog as before to verify that all previous E2E functionality still works. It will then need to log out to test the logout functionality as well.

Protractor Configuration

We already created a Protractor configuration file for the blog application in Chapter 5, and we've just moved that file into the MEAN application. The Protractor configuration file is shown here for reference:

```
/* chapter11/ conf.js Protractor configuration file */
```

```
exports.config = {
  seleniumAddress: 'http://localhost:4444/wd/hub',
  specs: ['e2e/blog-spec.js']
};
```

Protractor Test Specification

The modified Protractor test specification is shown next. Notice the new URL, as mentioned previously:

```
/* chapter11/blog-spec.js Protractor test specification */

describe("Blog Application Test", function(){
  it("should test the main blog page", function(){
    browser.get("http://localhost:8080/#!/");
    //logs into the blog application
    element(by.model("username")).sendKeys("node");
    element(by.model("password")).sendKeys("password");
    element(by.css('.form-button')).click();
    expect(browser.getTitle()).toEqual("AngularJS Blog");
    //gets the blog list
    var blogList = element.all(by.repeater('blogPost in blogList'));

    //test the size of the blogList
    expect(blogList.count()).toEqual(3);


    browser.get("http://localhost:8080/#!/blogPost/5387bafe185e4e972996adff");
    expect(browser.getTitle()).toEqual("AngularJS Blog");

    //gets the comment list
    var commentList = element.all(by.repeater('comment in blogEntry.comments'));

    //checks the size of the commentList
    expect(commentList.count()).toEqual(2);

    element(by.css('.navbar-brand')).click();

    //log out of the blog application
    element(by.id('lo')).click();
    expect(browser.getTitle()).toEqual("AngularJS Blog");
  });
});
```

Protractor Testing

We are now ready to start the end-to-end testing. Start a new command window and enter the following command to start the test server:

```
webdriver-manager start
```

Open a new command window and navigate to the root of the Chapter 11 project. Type the command:

```
protractor test/conf.js
```

You should see a browser window open. You should then see the test script log into the blog application and navigate through the pages of the application, as in Chapter 10. The script should then log out of the application. When the Protractor script has finished, the browser window will close.

You should see results like the following in the command window when the Protractor script completes. The number of seconds that it takes the script to finish will vary depending on your particular system:

```
Finished in 2.644 seconds
1 test, 5 assertions, 0 failures
```

We are now ready to continue with our deployment to the cloud.

MEAN Deployment to the Cloud

Now we will deploy our blog application to OpenShift using Git. NetBeans comes with a built-in version of Git that is very easy to configure and use when you're deploying to OpenShift. First you must open a free OpenShift account, which gives you three free gears (cloud server instances) that can run Node.js. Do the following:

1. Go to *https://www.openshift.com/app/account/new* and create a new account.

2. Click the "Add Application" button and create a new Node.js 0.10 application (save a copy of the page for reference later).

3. Add a MongoDB cartridge to the application (save a copy of the page for reference later).

4. Follow the OpenShift documentation and set up Git on your development environment. You'll need a public SSH key to use Git on the OpenShift system.

5. Once Git is configured, clone the application with Git to a location on your drive separate from the location where you unzipped the NodeBlog download.

6. Open the new OpenShift project, and copy the following files from the NodeBlog project to the new OpenShift project, replacing the existing versions:
   a. *package.json*
   b. *server.js*

7. Copy the *public* folder from the NodeBlog project to the new OpenShift project.

8. Copy the *db* folder from the NodeBlog project to the new OpenShift project.

Now we need to test the cloud version of the application locally. Open a command window and navigate to the folder where you placed the new OpenShift project. Make sure you see the *package.json* file, and enter `npm install` in the command window as you did earlier. Now right-click the OpenShift project and select "Run" from the menu. If you see the running indicator as shown before, the application is working properly.

Now, using the Git credentials that you set up earlier for your OpenShift application, do a Git remote push in NetBeans and the application will be deployed to OpenShift. If you see any errors, use the OpenShift documentation to resolve the error condition. Most problems are usually related to credentials and can be resolved easily.

Testing the Cloud Blog

Once the application is deployed to the cloud, open a browser and navigate to the OpenShift-supplied link for your application. If you didn't keep a copy of the application page, log in to your OpenShift account and click the application that you just created. The link to the application will be shown on the details pages.

Once you navigate to the link for your application, you should see the login screen as before. If you see the login screen, your application was successfully deployed to the cloud. Log in to your blog application and add a new blog post. Add a comment to the post. Your blog application should display the new post and the comment. If you would like to view the application logfiles, follow the OpenShift documentation related to viewing logfiles for more help.

This concludes our discussion on cloud deployment. Next, we'll take a brief look at how to turn your blog application into a mobile HTML5 application.

Mobile Version

The AngularJS blog application has all that we need to build a mobile version for any mobile platform. Our business logic is in the REST services, and all modern mobile devices can access REST services. We used a responsive design, so the application should look good on any mobile device. All modern mobile devices also have web browsers and native browser controls such as the Android `WebView` that can launch internal HTML pages.

The process for building a mobile blog application is straightforward for any mobile device. The process involves the following steps:

1. Create a new mobile project for the particular mobile device of choice.
2. Follow the Cordova documentation (*http://cordova.apache.org/*) and add Cordova to your mobile project.

3. Copy the entire contents of the Chapter 10 project (*AngularJsBlogChapter10*) to the folder in the mobile project specified by Cordova as a destination for HTML files for your particular mobile platform.

4. Follow the Cordova documentation and configure your mobile application to launch the *index.html* file copied from the Chapter 10 project.

5. Once the mobile project is configured according to the Cordova specifications, run the project on an emulator or a mobile device.

The application should run and look the same as the web version. There are no AngularJS-specific changes that we need to make to the project code. If you are interested in building AngularJS-based mobile applications, feel free to take the code from Chapter 10 and build a Cordova-based HTML5 mobile application for your platform of choice. The Cordova website (*http://cordova.apache.org/*) has documentation for all modern platforms to help you get started with your project.

Conclusion

In this chapter we made a few modifications and deployed our blog application to the cloud. We ran the application locally, and also ran the cloud-deployed application. We also took a quick look at how easy it is to build mobile applications with AngularJS. We will now focus on how to get your application found by search engines.

AngularJS and SEO

You might wonder why we are covering search engine optimization (SEO) in an AngularJS book. The answer is simple.

Currently, AngularJS and most JavaScript client-side frameworks are used mostly for web applications. Often, SEO is really not that important where web applications are concerned. As AngularJS gains in popularity, however, it could very well become a major player in the world of website design. AngularJS could potentially replace client-side code that is currently written in Java, PHP, Ruby, and Python.

That is not to say that those languages will be completely replaced—they won't. Java, PHP, Ruby, and Python will continue to be as important as ever in the world of software development, but in a different way. Those languages and their associated frameworks will take on the role of providing the backend REST services needed for AngularJS and other JavaScript client-side frameworks. When you consider that complete websites could soon be written with AngularJS, it's clear that SEO should then become a major concern for AngularJS developers. This chapter will help you to better understand AngularJS and SEO.

It is always best to focus more on building a great web application or website, and less on the specifics of search engines. Good design and performance are always by far the most important considerations for a new software project. Although search engine optimization is important, focusing too much on SEO during the design and implementation phase of a project can ultimately cost you valuable development hours.

Eventually, however, you do have to focus on getting your application or site found by all the major search engines. In this final chapter we will look at some of the ways to get your new AngularJS software found. Many of the practices presented here are recommended by Google.

Old Versus New AngularJS SEO

In the past, users of websites built with AngularJS had to follow a rather archaic process in which page snapshots were made for an entire site, and the website could then forward search engines to the snapshots so that they would see the prerendered version of the site rather than the actual JavaScript version of the site. Since conventional search engines didn't have the ability to execute JavaScript, pages built with AngularJS were rendered to older search engines as a blank white page with no content.

However, in a news release on May 23, 2014 (*http://bit.ly/1EWcX3P*), Google confirmed that it now has the capability to index JavaScript websites and applications. That is, the Googlebot has undergone upgrades to make it possible to index sites and applications that use Google's AngularJS and other JavaScript frameworks. For Google, that time-consuming and often expensive process of SEO for AngularJS is no longer necessary. Although the state of other search engines and their ability to execute JavaScript is unknown at this time, they will undoubtedly follow Google's lead very quickly, being forced to follow suit or get left behind.

There are also several companies that specialize in helping clients with the website prerendering process. Even though search engines are changing, many of these companies will doubtless continue offering prerendering services for several years, if you feel the need for those services.

Getting Found by Search Engines

With all that said, there are still some ways to increase your chances of getting a better ranking with Google and other search engines. We will cover the SEO tasks that are absolutely necessary:

1. Sign up for a Google Webmaster Tools account, add your site to the account, and follow Google's advice.
2. Build a *sitemap.xml* file for your site.
3. Add microformat tags to your site.
4. Make sure your JavaScript is clean and easy for search engines to execute.
5. Avoid calling REST services that take longer than two seconds to return results.

Google Webmaster Tools

One of the first things that you should do for SEO is to get a Google Webmaster Tools account. Once you add your site and start to follow Google's advice, you will see immediate improvements in your ranking and the number of pages of your site that are indexed by Google. The advice given by Google applies to other search engines as well. Don't expect to see SEO improvements drastically increase your ranking, however; SEO is an ongoing and time-consuming process that can take months or even years to render significant results.

Adding a Sitemap

According to Google, a sitemap file is very important to SEO. Google's Webmaster Tools will help you with the process of building a sitemap and uploading it to Google. Using a sitemap speeds up the process of getting your site indexed by making search engines aware of the pages and links on your site. You should keep the sitemap up-to-date, with any new pages added. Make sure to remove any pages from the sitemap that no longer exist on the site.

Microformat Tags

Another thing that improves SEO is the use of microformat tags (tag-based navigation). The use of tag-based navigation started on blog sites but has spread considerably over the last few years; it is now used on business websites as well.

Tag-based navigation uses the format shown here to indicate to search engines that the page content contains the related keywords. As you can see, the href attribute contains a link to a page on the site, and the rel attribute tells search engines that the page contains the referenced keywords:

```
<!-- chapter12/ tag-based navigation -->

<p> Tags: <a href="http://www.ulboracms.org/#!/" rel="tag">Ulbora CMS</a>,
<a href="http://www.ulboracms.org/#!/" rel="tag">Java CMS</a>,
<a href="http://www.ulboracms.org/#!/" rel="tag">REST service</a>,
<a href="http://www.ulboracms.org/#!/" rel="tag">JSON REST</a>,
<a href="http://
www.ulboracms.org/#!/article/26" rel="tag">REST web services</a></p>
```

Tag-based navigation is supported by all major search engines.

Building Clean Client Code

One of the best ways to improve SEO is to create a clean and efficient AngularJS application. Unnecessary JavaScript should always be avoided. JavaScript methods should execute quickly, with no unnecessary processes running in the background.

Search engines take page speed into consideration when ranking sites. Pages that contain long-running JavaScript functions may get dropped by Google and other search engines and not get indexed. Once a page gets dropped by a search engine, it can take a long time to get that page indexed again.

Building Fast REST Services

One last thing that can directly affect page speed and SEO is the speed of the REST web services used to populate page content. Pages that rely on slow REST services can suffer as a result. REST services should return results in two seconds or less.

Services that return results in under a second are best for SEO and site performance. Although REST service design is beyond the scope of this particular book, I want to emphasize how important web service design is to SEO when web pages rely on those services for content. When your site depends on REST services, always make sure those services perform well and add no unnecessary delay to your site or application. Always insist on peak-performing services.

Conclusion

That brings us to the end of this chapter and the end of the book. I've done my best to present AngularJS in a way that will make it easy to understand for both beginners and experienced developers alike. The concept of using JavaScript client-side frameworks to build complete frontend applications and websites is relatively new, and often referred to as "cutting edge" by many. The recent Google announcement related to JavaScript and SEO mentioned earlier attests to that.

But things that are considered cutting edge today will be commonplace in a few years. I believe AngularJS will be at the forefront of application development in coming years, and is well worth the time spent learning the framework. This book is only a starting point, however. Now you must go out and develop great applications with AngularJS, and have fun building those applications too! Remember, the best AngularJS application is a well-designed AngularJS application. Always build the best applications that you possibly can. It's worth the effort in the end.

References

- AngularJS (*https://angularjs.org/*)
- Bootstrap (*http://getbootstrap.com/*)
- jQuery (*http://jquery.com/*)
- Wikipedia entry for MVC (*http://bit.ly/mvc-wiki*)
- Wikipedia entry for REST (*http://bit.ly/restful_web_services*)
- Wikipedia entry for Web service (*http://bit.ly/wiki-web-service*)
- Ulbora CMS (*http://www.ulboracms.org*)
- Ulbora CMS at SourceForge (*http://bit.ly/dl-ulbora*)
- Wikipedia entry for SPA (*http://bit.ly/dwc-spa*)
- Wikipedia entry for RWD (*http://bit.ly/wiki-rwd*)

Index

Symbols

$location service, 139
$rootScope object, 89
$scope object, 7
    adding behavior to, 39
    attaching methods to, 139
    models in, 89
<select> element (HTML), 164
{{}} (double curly braces), 8

A

Active Server Pages (ASP), 23
Ajax
    REST services and, 78
    sites, 6
AngularJS
    as client-side framework, 1
    as MVC framework, 27
    bootstrapping with, 3
    business logic in, 8
    controllers, 7
    dependency injection, 4
    directives, 121-135
    downloading files for, 11
    HTML compiler, 121
    HTML5 and, 5
    integrating with other frameworks, 9
    model classes, 7
    routes, 4
    search engines and, 6
    SEO for, 181-184
    services, non-REST, 104
    single-page applications in, 2
    templates, 6
    testing, 9
    view classes in, 7
Apache Cordova, 179
applications
    adding service modules to, 94
    running in IDEs, 15, 69
    running with models, 97
    testing in IDEs, 15-21
    transportable, 159
    using REST services in, 92
ASP.NET framework, 1
authentication, 103-108

B

Basic Authentication, 104, 163
bootstrapping, 3
    HTML code and, 13
business logic, 103-119
    adding to projects, 108-111
    controller, 41
    in controllers, 8
    REST services and, 77
    user authentication, 103-108
    using, 110

C

CakePHP framework, 24
    integrating with AngularJS, 9
callback functions, 82
cascading style sheets, 65
Chrome Developer Tools, 97
client code, 183
client-side frameworks, 1
    integrating AngularJS with, 9

About the Author

Ken Williamson is a software engineer and architect with over twenty years of experience in the technology industry. Ken's first programming language was Assembly using the 6502 chip. He moved on to C and C++ and eventually to Java and JavaScript. Ken has designed and written mobile, desktop, and server software for some of the biggest companies in the world.

Ken holds a BS in Computer Science from Kennesaw State University. He is the founder of several open source projects including Ulbora CMS; he has also contributed to many other open source projects over the years. Ken makes his home in Atlanta, Georgia with his wife, Sherry. You can find Ken at *www.ken-williamson.com*.

Colophon

The animals on the cover of *Learning AngularJS* are Florida cricket frogs (*Acris gryllus dorsalis*), which are subspecies of the Southern cricket frog. They can be found all throughout Florida, with the exception of the extreme northwestern panhandle.

Cricket frogs prefer a freshwater environment, such as puddles, lakes, marshes, and streams. They are easily recognized by the triangular mark on their heads and the two dark stripes on their rear.

Breeding occurs from April into the fall, with small clusters of eggs attached to submerged plants. Males advertise their readiness with a loud, rapid call of *gick, gick, gick*, which has been described by some as the sound of marbles clicking together.

Adult Florida cricket frogs grow to be about 1.25 inches long, and vary in color from dark brown to tan or green. They enjoy healthy population growth and are not considered threatened in any way.

Many of the animals on O'Reilly covers are endangered; all of them are important to the world. To learn more about how you can help, go to *animals.oreilly.com*.

The cover image is from Lydekker's *Royal Natural History*. The cover fonts are URW Typewriter and Guardian Sans. The text font is Adobe Minion Pro; the heading font is Adobe Myriad Condensed; and the code font is Dalton Maag's Ubuntu Mono.

Get even more for your money.

Join the O'Reilly Community, and register the O'Reilly books you own. It's free, and you'll get:

- $4.99 ebook upgrade offer
- 40% upgrade offer on O'Reilly print books
- Membership discounts on books and events
- Free lifetime updates to ebooks and videos
- Multiple ebook formats, DRM FREE
- Participation in the O'Reilly community
- Newsletters
- Account management
- 100% Satisfaction Guarantee

Signing up is easy:

1. Go to: oreilly.com/go/register
2. Create an O'Reilly login.
3. Provide your address.
4. Register your books.

Note: English-language books only

To order books online:
oreilly.com/store

For questions about products or an order:
orders@oreilly.com

To sign up to get topic-specific email announcements and/or news about upcoming books, conferences, special offers, and new technologies:
elists@oreilly.com

For technical questions about book content:
booktech@oreilly.com

To submit new book proposals to our editors:
proposals@oreilly.com

O'Reilly books are available in multiple DRM-free ebook formats. For more information:
oreilly.com/ebooks

O'REILLY®

Have it your way.

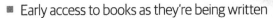

CPSIA information can be obtained at www.ICGtesting.com
Printed in the USA
LVOW03s2322180915

454769LV00027B/124/P